Help for the Struggling Student

·····································

READY-TO-USE STRATEGIES AND LESSONS TO BUILD ATTENTION, MEMORY, & ORGANIZATIONAL SKILLS

Mimi Gold

JOSSEY-BASS
A Wiley Imprint
www.josseybass.com

Published by Jossey-Bass
A Wiley Imprint
989 Market Street, San Francisco, CA 94103-1741   www.josseybass.com

Jossey-Bass books and products are available through most bookstores. To contact Jossey-Bass directly, call our Customer Care Department within the U.S. at (800) 956-7739, outside the U.S. at (317) 572-3993 or fax (317) 572-4002.

Jossey-Bass also publishes its books in a variety of electronic formats. Some content that appears in print may not be available in electronic books.

Permission granted by Dover Publications, Inc., to reprint worksheets on pages 91 through 95.

Library of Congress Cataloging-in-Publication Data

Gold, Mimi, 1943–
    Help for the struggling student : ready-to-use strategies and lessons
to build attention, memory, and organizational skills / Mimi Gold.—1st
ed.
        p.   cm.
    ISBN 0-7879-6588-X (pbk. : alk. paper)
    1. Learning-disabled children—Education.   2. Individualized
instruction.   3. Study skills.   I. Title.
    LC4704.G65 2003
    371.39'4—dc21

                                        2003001796

Printed in the United States of America
FIRST EDITION
PB Printing 10 9 8 7 6 5 4 3 2 1

Dedication

To all the students who willingly talked about their learning frustrations and shared their personal solutions for specific difficulties. Their ability to create imaginative and effective compensatory strategies was a wonder to behold. Without them this book would not exist.

Acknowledgments

If we are lucky in our lifetime, we encounter special people who force us to stretch beyond our perceived limits and reach for a dream. Over the years Dr. Robin Morris persisted in reminding me that I could and must write about how to teach the struggling student. In my search for a publisher, Dr. Robin Cooper continuously guided me through the maze of decisions I needed to make. Friends forever, better known as the "Hard Core" and the "Woo Woo's," patiently encouraged me as I repeatedly announced that I was writing a book that stopped and started. Family, which includes artists, nurses, physical therapists, writers, and technology experts, were always available to share their expertise or be there when I desperately needed a boost to keep moving forward. Especially dear students like Brandon, Whitney, Abby, and Tiffany and their parents led me to believe how important it is to share what I have learned. Watching my daughter, Fara, who naturally took risks without lengthy pauses, made me realize that anything was possible, if only you believe. What a model she has become. Finally, but most important, a million thanks to Susan Kolwicz, Bernice Golden, Win Huppuch, and Nancy Kennedy, formerly at Prentice Hall. They are the best editorial team anyone could ever have asked for. Their highly knowledgeable guidance and patience with my endless questions are forever appreciated.

About the Author

Mimi Gold is presently the School Program Coordinator for children and adolescents who are hospitalized in the Rehabilitation Departments of Children's Healthcare of Atlanta, Georgia. Prior to this position, she was a Cognitive Specialist in the Georgia State University Brain Injury Project. She has an extensive background in general and special education, teaching students of all ages who are gifted or have learning disabilities, health impairments, physical impairments, or neurological impairments.

Ms. Gold holds a Bachelor of Science degree from Duquesne University in Pittsburgh, Pennsylvania and a Master's degree in Human Development and Learning Disabilities from Pacific Oaks College in Pasadena, California. She has been a visiting professor in the education departments of both institutions.

She is an active member of the Council for Exceptional Children and the Brain Injury Association and has presented workshops and papers at meetings of both these organizations. Ms. Gold has conducted numerous inservice teacher workshops offered by county school systems and regional learning resource centers throughout the state of Georgia. She has presented workshops on such topics as Instructional Strategies for the Regular Classroom, Learning Strategies for the Attention Deficit Student, Special Needs of the Brain Injured Student, and School Re-entry after a Brain Injury.

The demand for materials from participants in her workshops became the impetus for creating this book.

About This Resource

This is a resource book of learning strategies, or solutions, for the teacher or parent who is trying to help a struggling student. Students are considered to be struggling when they have the potential to learn but are frustrated by difficulties that interfere with their overall performance. Learning strategies that show students how to approach tasks in new ways can reduce or eliminate their frustrations and enable them to complete tasks more successfully. By expanding the number of strategies available to students, instructors can help them become more independent and successful learners.

The strategies presented in this book are grouped into three sections that correspond with the three global components of learning: attention, memory, and organization. These three components are the "networks" through which the brain actually processes, or interprets, new information a student is attempting to learn. Each section of the book begins with a general description of the learning behaviors that are performed by that specific component of learning. In addition, each section provides numerous ready-to-use visuals, sample tasks, "recipes," model dialogues, and worksheets to help instructors implement the strategies.

This book also provides essential information about how to observe students as they perform learning tasks and how to recognize when a new strategy would be helpful. It is important to know if a strategy matches a student's personal style of learning. To teach strategies at random without considering a student's individual needs can increase the student's frustration. Thus, the purpose of this book is threefold:

1. To provide information about how to identify a student's personal learning style

2. To provide guidance in selecting strategies for the specific student, based on his or her learning style and needs

3. To provide a range of strategies to help students become more effective, independent, and successful learners

To help students better understand how to use a strategy, numerous illustrations are included. For students, a picture is truly worth a thousand words. Presenting a picture cue card for a strategy—prior to instruction—greatly improves students' understanding and reduces the need for excessive wording in instructions. Best of all, the pictures can be copied, cut out, and placed near the students' work area to remind them to use the strategy. The pictures can also be enlarged for display on bulletin boards or chart stands. In this way, the teacher or parent can simply walk over to a chart or bulletin board and point to it as a reminder.

Strategies can be selected to enhance students' strengths or to compensate for a weakness. By using the provided sample tasks, instructors can actively model how to employ a given strategy to complete an activity or worksheet. The sample tasks can be enlarged and reproduced, or copied on the board for teachers to complete with students. Given many opportunities for guided practice and consistent praise for their efforts, students will begin to internalize the strategy and use it independently, thus improving their performance on school-related tasks.

At the beginning of each strategy, there is a description of a specific student's frustrated behavior as he or she approaches a learning task. Instructors may want to read all the "Observed Behavior" descriptions first, especially if they have a particular student in mind. These behavior descriptions are included to help teachers and parents recognize their own students' behaviors. That "ah ha . . . sounds like Tommy" feeling clearly helps the teacher or parent identify the strategy or strategies that are most likely to be helpful.

Many students naturally develop key strategies for building attention, memory, and organizational skills that promote learning. However, for the struggling student, such automatic strategic thinking, or problem solving, may not develop independently. Instead, these children often require the guidance of an insightful teacher or parent who carefully observes a pattern of repeated frustrations. In that instant of recognizing the problem, instructors can begin to determine what strategy may reduce the problem—or possibly eliminate it altogether! By providing students with specific strategies, improvements in academic performance can be achieved.

It is my hope that the strategies presented in this book can help the struggling students—especially the students in your class or your home—to become successful learners. It has been my experience over the past 25 years that students do learn when they have the tools they need to help themselves. What a joy it is to help them discover just the right tools. May you hear more "ah ha's" this year than ever before!

Mimi Gold

Contents

. . . .

Section Two: Attention-Enhancing Strategies

Section Three: Memory-Enhancing Strategies

VISUAL-LEARNER STRATEGIES

PAIRED-MEMORY-LEARNER STRATEGIES

MULTIMODALITY-LEARNER STRATEGIES

Section Four: Organization-Enhancing Strategies

READING STRATEGIES

MATH STRATEGIES

WRITTEN-LANGUAGE STRATEGIES

Section One

How Students Learn

•••

Learning Styles

What Should We Understand Before Attempting to Help a Struggling Student?

When, after repeated attempts, a struggling student still fails to learn, a frustrated teacher may resort to trying the latest new tool just because everyone has said, "It's fantastic." Yet without careful consideration of how the new tool is designed to work, we may be putting the student at risk for yet another failure if the approach used by the new tool does not match the student's particular style of learning. Students have unique ways to learn that usually prove to be easier and more successful for them. If the help offered is to be effective and have a lasting impact, discovering a struggling student's preferred way of learning is essential.

What Is a Learning Style? Why Is It Important?

A student's preferred way of learning is called a *learning style*. This means that, given a choice, a student would have a preference for how new information should be presented and how it should be organized for study.

There are many theories on what a learning style should consist of, but all of them include the need for an understanding of the primary senses of the body for perceiving information. We can take in information through our eyes, ears, muscles/joints, and skin:

- Knowledge gained and mastered through our visual system is called our *visual memory*.

- Knowledge gained and mastered through our hearing system is called our *verbal* or *auditory memory*.

- Knowledge gained and mastered through our muscle system is called our *motor* or *kinesthetic memory*.

- Knowledge gained and mastered through our skin system is called our *tactile memory*. Obviously, it is difficult to separate skin from muscle, so we may hear the last two terms used interchangeably and often labeled as *tactile-kinesthetic memory*.

Most learners prefer one sensory channel, or mode, to the others, as it is easier for them to understand or remember information through that particular sensory channel. We each develop unique storage, or memory, systems to keep track of the information we take in with our senses. If we store the new information in our brain "our way," we will usually be able to retrieve it more easily at a later time.

When we are taught in our preferred mode, or style, we can learn with less effort. As adults, most of us can describe how we successfully learn, study, and become adept at a new skill. Knowing our learning style enables us, as adults, to choose consciously what to do in a frustrating or challenging moment in order to improve our performance. For example, when learning a new computer software program, we might read an instruction manual, take a class that encourages "hands-on" learning, ask someone else to give us pointers, talk ourselves through the process, or draw pictures to illustrate concepts. Yet, someone observing our learning behaviors may have difficulty identifying exactly what we are doing that makes it easier for us to learn. So, in order to be effective, we must discover how to observe and identify a student's learning style, but we also must remember to <u>ask the student</u> to describe what he or she is doing that we cannot observe.

What Is the First Step in Identifying a Student's Learning Style?

An understanding of learning style is based on recognizing when something seems easy to learn or difficult to learn. That something can be an academic subject area, a particular skill, a hobby, or an activity. We can recognize our learning style by noticing what is fun for us—something we really like to do—because it is easy; it comes naturally. In that "fun" activity, what are the essential parts of the task that we seem to do without a great deal of thinking? These parts just seem to be second nature to us. We don't need to exert much energy; the energy just flows without stressful effort.

As adults, we also are aware that it is difficult to observe what others might be doing mentally to maximize their performance. This is true as well when observing students, but it is complicated by their age and/or lack of experience. Students generally do not know what their learning preference, or style, is until they near the middle of elementary school, somewhere between the ages of 8 and 10. (We must keep in mind, however, that, as with all developmental milestones, individual children may reach this stage earlier or later than the norm suggests.)

The field of neuropsychology, which studies developmental brain behaviors, has labeled this stage of brain development, when we can self-choose how to learn, as "metacognitive ability," or the ability to think about our own thinking processes. Up until that time, young students can be trained to learn techniques that improve their performance on tasks, but they cannot normally analyze their own frustrations and come up with solutions while performing a task. Tools for learning are accumulated in the early years of schooling by watching adults model ways to learn and through direct instruction on how to carry out a specific action that improves learning. Over time, students begin to recognize that certain ways of doing a task and of being taught are personally more effective, thereby resulting in greater success.

In observing students, we must first be able to notice what, when, and how they learn or remember without excessive effort or study. What types of information do they excel at? In what subjects do they perform well? What types of activities do they choose? What is it in the activity—at a very basic sensory skill level of seeing, feeling, touching, hearing, talking, moving, and so on—that the student seems to do instinctively or effortlessly?

What Kinds of Behaviors Indicate a Preference for Seeing, Hearing, Touching, or Moving?

As observers of learning style, we can begin to interpret our observations by noticing students' most obvious choices for listening, looking, touching, and moving. To efficiently notice these "telling" behaviors, we must observe very carefully, as small details in students' behaviors can be very important. For example, as you hand students a story to read, watch their reactions. Do they jump right into the reading of it or do they immediately explore the illustrations? Carefully watch where their eyes are looking. The students who jump right into reading are using *listening*—they hear the words in their minds to get the information into their verbal memory systems. The students who explore illustrations are using *looking*—they gather the story meaning through pictures to get the information into their visual memory systems.

A similar example would be to watch students as they are given a worksheet to complete. Do students actually read the directions or do they seem to scan the printed layout of a task to figure out how to do it? Direction readers are obviously using their words, which is just "listening in print," or their hearing system. They are using their verbal memory skills to understand the task. Scanners, however, are using their memory of how a task is laid out visually in print on the page to interpret the task. They are choosing to use their visual memory skills to understand the task. Scanners know, for example, that they don't have to read the directions for a matching task to understand what to do, because the task is usually set up in visually parallel columns. An observer can watch students' eye movements as they scan a page or their mouth movements as they read to pick up these clues. Direction readers often read in whispered voices or with lip movements, so they can hear the "echo" of their own voices to monitor the accuracy of what they read. Direction readers often can be observed using their fingers to track under lines of print. This increases their attention to the words.

As students study a list of terms, do they say the words to themselves, spell the words out loud, write them again, illustrate them, or make cards for matching them? All of these behaviors are examples of students making personal choices about how they prefer to react to a task or what they have found has worked in the past. Speakers or spellers are likely using their listening, or verbal memory. Students who rewrite to study probably are using both their verbal word memory and their motor movement memory. Illustrators are activating their visual image memory, and possibly their motor memory, in the process of drawing. Often, students who look off into "space" as they think are seeing pictures in their minds of the ideas they are studying. They are activating their visual skills in the form of mental movies, or visualizations. Students who benefit from studying with card matching likely are using their muscles and skin to combine motor and kinesthetic memory. The movement needed in reaching to match items may also increase memory. Notice, however, that each of these studying students has to look at the words, so they each may be focusing on what they see to build their visual memory.

As these examples reveal, many learners prefer to have the information come into their minds by pairing two sets of sensory information. This paired sensory learning style also can be seen in the additional examples that follow. One student might best remember a lecture by actively listening, using only his verbal memory; another student may need to take lots of notes so she can "see" the lecture better with her visual memory of printed words as she listens. Sometimes, students can also be found drawing illustrations for concepts as they listen to instruction. At first glance, you might think they are doodling. Yet on closer inspection, you will notice that the doodles are actually illustrations of the words heard during your lecture. These students are using visual memory to enhance their listening. Some students don't "get it" from a lecture or a text reading unless they can act it out or use three-dimensional materials that can be moved to experience the lecture's concept. Students' use of a secondary sensory input can enhance the quality of their learning.

How Can We Begin to Interpret Our Observations of a Student's Learning?

Once an instructor becomes aware of the value of careful observation, it may be quite simple to notice what the struggling student is doing with ease, or with little effort. However, that is not enough. Instructors must be able to understand and carefully interpret what they are observing—not just the act itself, but also all the small pieces of the behavior. Maybe there are parts of an activity that a student does well or does poorly. Why are some parts easy as compared with those that are difficult? How do we break down a task into parts so we can understand what is easy or hard for a given student?

As instructors, it is our job to help the students recognize when and why something is hard or easy. Helping students recognize why a task is "easier" leads to an awareness of their own personal learning style. Initially, this will require that we help students to remember what they were actually doing or thinking when they were successful on a particular task. By combining our observation with the students' personal descriptions of what they think they are doing, we are able to define more clearly what is happening in that moment.

Using "hindsight" thinking *immediately* after completing a successful task enables students to recall more accurately what they did to help themselves. Most students do not know how to explain what they did, so we must provide assistance and offer some descriptions of what they *might have been doing*. If we ask them some leading questions, they might recognize what their brain was doing. Hindsight questioning with students might include some of these questions:

- What made you remember that?
- Did you remember writing it on the paper?
- Did you see in your mind the words actually printed on the study paper?
- Could you see it printed on a particular part of the page?
- Did you hear yourself saying the words last night as you studied?
- Did you hear someone else say it, such as Mom, Dad, the teacher, or a friend or classmate?
- Did you remember the place where you learned it?
- Did you remember the illustration on the page?
- Did you see a picture in your mind for the answer?
- Did you feel yourself moving your hands or feet as you learned it?

Remember to pause between questions. This is important because it provides the student "thinking time" to consider each idea.

As instructors, we can help students to find the words they can use to describe what they did to help themselves. Sometimes we may also be able to demonstrate what students did to help themselves because it was observable. However, by employing the students' ideas as well as our own observations, we will be better able to help them recognize their special techniques and thus repeat them on another occasion.

Realistically, we cannot be there all the time to notice what students are doing. However, whatever time we can expend helping students examine and discuss what they do well is absolutely invaluable to them. Each time we identify the same technique being used or encourage a student to use one that is very effective, we help that student to build a set of memorable reasons for choosing a specific behavior for completing a task. Thus, each time the student experiences success using a particular approach, he or she builds a stronger sense of how to respond to challenging tasks and how to complete them with increasing ease.

Only through careful observation and direct discussion with their students can instructors get a clear picture of what students are doing to help themselves. When working with struggling students, we must find time to ask them what they do and combine this information with our observations. Given time and careful instruction, students can discover their own unique way of learning. When this unique way of learning becomes the student's active learning style, he or she will become more self-aware, selecting effective tools and techniques in varied situations.

Thinking Styles

How Can We Observe Differences in Thinking Styles?

Instructors can observe preferences by noticing the quality of students' performances when they are doing tasks that demand specific ways of thinking or reasoning. Different types of thinkers process information in different ways.

There are two general types of thinkers: synthesizers and analyzers. Both of these types know the results they want; they just employ different kinds of logic and use different skill sets to accomplish their goals. *Synthesizers* work backward from the whole. They don't follow the expected "rules." They see the "big" picture clearly and then figure out their own way to create it. These "whole thinkers" tend to prefer working with their visual memory. To them, a picture is truly worth a thousand words. For example, given instructions to construct an object, they may end up with a very creative adaptation that often defies explanation. Yet, this often does not concern them because they thrive on clever or unusual thinking.

By contrast, *analyzers* figure out how to construct the object one step at a time in logical order. They prefer a "recipe" approach for creating the object. They must have all the component pieces and the instructions before they can see or understand the finished product. You can almost hear them thinking, "First, I should do this . . . and then. . . ." They must consider all the small details to obtain the perfect end-product. These students are sequential learners, who usually prefer to learn through their verbal memory.

The Synthesizer

Before they can begin a task, synthesizers need to know the end result. Synthesizers cannot perform easily without a sense of the final product or expectation. So, all instruction for a synthesizer would be more efficient if the instructor provided an overview, or preview. If you were to watch synthesizers building a model, you would see them pause to consider the overall design. If there happened to be instructions available, synthesizers would most likely ignore them. Instead, they would rapidly build the object without paying any attention to the order in which they constructed the parts. Synthesizers enjoy the end result, even if it does not quite match the original design, because they know the value of being different.

The Analyzer

Analyzers, by contrast, would use the instructions to build the model. They would carefully follow each step sequentially, believing that if they didn't, they would not be able to create the object. If analyzers should get stuck in their construction, they could benefit from asking the synthesizer for help. Keep in mind that synthesizers would not be able to explain it in words, but they could show analyzers how to fix the object so it "looked" right.

How Can We Identify Synthesizers and Analyzers in School Tasks?

Generally speaking, *synthesizers* excel in skills that require an understanding of space and quantity. In particular, they are good at mathematics. Often, these students can be observed internally computing number problems with ease. It's only when the teacher forces them to follow "rules," or steps, for calculation on paper-and-pencil math that these students get frustrated. They know the answer, but get confused with the details, or order, of writing it down on paper. Frequently, synthesizers become excellent artists and designers. Scale drawings, plans, or constructions—though tedious for some—typically are hobbies of the synthesizer. They tend to be good at sports and remember more easily what they have seen than what they have heard.

As readers, they depend on creating a mental image of the story line, characters, and settings. They use sentence context to understand what they are reading. When they stumble on an unknown word, they often substitute an alternative that fits the context of the sentence. This strategy makes up for their normally weaker skills in decoding unknown words that appear in the story. The skill of decoding, or sounding out words, requires an ability to hear the sounds of letters in a specific order or sequence. Synthesizers normally do not master decoding without creative instruction because they encounter difficulty in blending together a string of appropriate sounds when they see a sequence of letters. This obviously affects their spelling ability, but they may also possess the ability to look at their written words and notice when they look "funny." They are using their visual memory of the whole word to recognize an incorrect word, but they often cannot correct the word, even when they know it is wrong.

Analyzers, on the other hand, are generally good speakers, readers, writers, and spellers. They thrive in situations where they can think of things in a logical order. They easily learn to interpret unknown words as they read because they are experts at blending a series of letter sounds together into a recognizable word. However, this sound-blending skill is not always so effective in their spelling because they depend on spelling exactly what they hear as they slowly say the word parts. As a majority of words in our English language do not follow expected pronunciation rules, analyzers can make spelling errors. They must develop visual memory skills for how words actually "look" rather than depend completely on how words "sound."

Reading comprehension demands that we read each sentence and change the mental picture of the events or characters in our mind to include new information as we read on. Sentence by sentence, we must add or change details, so that a series of "slides" are constructed for the ongoing story. Analyzers are good at building story comprehension sequentially, word by word, sentence by sentence, and paragraph by paragraph. The end result is a complete story "tape" that can be "reheard" in their minds.

Analyzers also tend to be adept at writing stories because they can organize thoughts in a logical, step-by-step order. However, their original drafts for writing, though very exact and descriptive, may not be so clever or imaginative as those of synthesizers, who love creative and unusual ideas.

Mathematically, analyzers are usually good at paper-and-pencil calculation. This is because they perform well when they have to follow a step-by-step procedure, and many calculations demand complex, sequentially ordered procedures to achieve accuracy. Analyzers also are good at interpreting word problems because they can attack the problem one sentence at a time. However, they may have difficulty with interpreting spatial analysis problems, such as those found in geometry, that demand an understanding of what the end-point solution should "look like." They must scribble or draw their possible solutions on paper to determine the correct sequence for reaching the end-point solution. This is the opposite of the synthesizers, who easily see the whole geometry problem in their minds and usually can estimate the answer without knowing how they did it.

How Can a Student's Ability Level Affect His or Her Thinking Style?

When students have an identified learning problem compounded by a below-average ability level, their use of reasoning as a tool for new learning may be affected. This does not mean that they will not benefit from discovering their personal learning style. It also does not mean that we should assume they don't have special ways of learning. However, it does demand that we explore varied possibilities for practice.

Slower learners, even those who do not have an easily discerned strength area for learning, can benefit from practice. Once a skill is learned, these students can then be shown specific situations in which their newly learned technique could be applied to improve their performance. This type of learning style has been called "rote learning." With practice and review, these students can persist in mastering new ways to perform tasks successfully. Obviously, their instructors will need to be creative in developing interesting ways to review, or the students may give up. Games and computer programs that incorporate practice of a new skill can be highly motivating.

The learning and review of a new skill may also need to be broken down into the smaller pieces. For example, to encourage the use of tactile-kinesthetic memory for counting accurately in basic addition, students could practice adding only "one more" to each number tower of cubes to master the facts for all the "plus ones" in adding. The students would feel and see the increasing value of adding one more. Once this was mastered, the students could then count "two more" to each number tower for the "plus twos" in adding. Charting their small successes with the "plus ones and twos" may give them the positive feedback they need to see that the practice is worth the effort. Such motivational systems can be very effective to ensure that they persist with their practicing.

Do Students Have to Learn Using Only Their Personal Learning Style?

As instructors, we must not limit instruction to the student's preferred learning style. Although each student will have a preference, he or she can benefit from being taught different approaches for mastering new information. By being exposed to new ways to learn, students will possibly add to their learning repertoire. However, when they become frustrated learning a new technique, it may be time to remind them of their usual way of completing this kind of task.

We must carefully observe our students as they perform learning tasks. While observing, we will notice when they are successful and which skills and strategies they employ to achieve success. However, we are not always able to see evidence of their mental processes as they work through problems. Without encouraging their participation in our analysis, we may not have all the information we need. So, we must give them the opportunity to tell us what they think they are doing as they successfully perform tasks. Using a team approach in which we respect and include their ideas, we will identify more accurately the strategies that students are employing successfully as well as unearth relevant strategies that may be missing. By building students' awareness of how they learn most effectively and by teaching them additional strategies needed to compensate for weaknesses, we help them discover their entire, or global, learning style. Our job as instructors is to lead them to understand how they can best:

- Take in the information through a preferred sensory channel.
- Use specific strategies that help strengthen their learning in areas of weakness.

- Remember and retrieve learned information and efficiently express their knowledge.
- Use their thinking style as synthesizers or analyzers in order to complete complex tasks systematically.

In helping students recognize their individual ways of learning, we provide them with at least one approach they can count on. That one way ensures that, when all else fails, they will be able to learn new information and remember it successfully. When students can activate a personal learning style, they will become more confident, more flexible, and more open to new ideas.

Strategies

How Are Strategies Different from Learning and Thinking Styles?

Now that we know about learning and thinking styles, why do we need to know about strategies? How are strategies different from learning and thinking styles? Learning and thinking styles may not always serve us perfectly. For example, our learning style may have some imperfections, or glitches, that can interfere with the quality of our learning. These "glitches" may create moments of visible frustration. When we become frustrated by our inability to continue successfully, we need a way to proceed—a strategy—that will get us past the difficulty. Therefore, strategies are techniques that are used in conjunction with students' individual learning and thinking styles to maximize their performance.

There are two general purposes for strategies. A strategy can be a tool we use to compensate for weaknesses, or it can be a tool we use to enhance strengths. Regardless of the reason for using it, a strategy should enrich the quality of students' performance in conjunction with their individual learning and thinking styles.

What Can Strategies Do for a Struggling Student?

While observing students' strengths, we should take special note when an otherwise successful performance hits a frustration point. Usually, the students will not know how to deal with the difficulty; hence their frustrations. This is where we should step in to offer guidance. There are many different kinds of difficulties and many different strategies for solving them. Careful observation, brainstorming with students, and increased experience over time will help instructors to become more adept at knowing which strategy might be effective in a specific situation with a specific student.

What Are Some Observable "Glitches" and Their Corresponding Strategies?

Typically, there are observable behaviors that indicate students may be having difficulty. They may pause in the midst of a task, or grimace, or even stop working. In these situations, students often call out for help. Most commonly, students are stuck on a part of a task rather than confused by the entire task. They have hit a "glitch" and a strategy for dealing with it is needed. Some examples of typical "glitches" follow.

Difficulty Recalling Specific Word Meanings

Many students experience this "glitch" while reading. The student appears to be a good reader, yet—when asked specific questions related to vocabulary after reading—he or she is unable to explain the meaning of a word that was used throughout the story. We know that reading stories does not demand that the reader know the exact meaning of all words. He or she can guess the meaning of many words by using context clues within the sentence and surrounding text. Readers can even skip some words and still follow the flow of the story to get the main ideas. Yet, because students often are expected to recall and understand the meanings of words in detail, they will need some strategies to help them. There are a number of strategies that might be useful. For example, the students can be taught to make a small dot or mark on the line in which an unfamiliar word appears. Then they can go back later and ask someone else to explain the word without interrupting the flow of reading.

Difficulty Differentiating Between Similar Letters

Students frequently experience this "glitch" when they write certain letters. They have trouble figuring out which letter is "b" and which is "d." They have to stop and look up at an alphabet letter strip that hangs in the front of the classroom. Looking up and down from their paper to the letter strip causes them to become confused visually, but it does help them figure out which letter is which. Would these students benefit from a strategy that provides meaningful pictures that match the exact shape of letters? They could then more easily recall the appropriate picture to help them identify the letter. The pictures could be mounted on their desks or placed in a reading folder until they were mastered.

Difficulty Retaining Ideas When Writing Paragraphs

This "glitch" occurs to many students in story or paragraph writing. They can think of good ideas for their sentences, but cannot remember their ideas long enough to get them down on paper. The physical requirements of handwriting combined with the mental job of monitoring word order cause them to lose track of the idea they had in their minds just moments ago. What if we could encourage them to whisper the sentence to themselves, or "self-talk" as they are writing? What if, when they get stuck in the middle of a sentence, they learn to reread aloud what they have written so far in order to retrieve the lost idea? Wouldn't they possibly be more successful?

How Do We Teach a Strategy?

Once the instructor has chosen the strategy most appropriate for helping a specific situation, it must be modeled while the students observe. For the students to understand, the instructors will need to *role-play*. They will pretend to do the same frustrating task, solving the problem with the chosen strategy. Students often benefit from hearing instructors "think aloud," or describe what they are doing as the task is performed. Sometimes, the strategy is a mental act that students cannot observe but the instructor can describe aloud. A spoken description of what the instructor is thinking as he or she does the task is very important so the students can see and hear the strategy simultaneously. After the strategy has been modeled, the students should perform it, copying the instructor's presentation. Then the instructor can determine if the students actually understood how to use the strategy. If the students did not understand, the instructor can repeat the same scenario or do it again with new material. Initially, the students will need reminders to use the demonstrated strategy at times when it will be helpful. A picture illustration of the new strategy can be placed on the students' desks to remind them to use it. Students need to be encouraged to use a new strategy. It is highly motivating to students to hear the instructor's praise every time they use the strategy, even if they had to be reminded to do so.

Often, students learn a strategy in one environment, or with a particular task, and they do not realize that it can be used somewhere else. Reminders about strategies are also effective when students are distracted by their internal thoughts, or by environmental sounds or sights, and do not recognize an opportunity to use the strategy. The trick is to know how, when, and where to remind students, with a minimum of negative attention. Copying strategy illustrations or recipes and placing them in the students' work areas is a subtle but effective means of reminding them to use a strategy. Short telegraphic statements like "Rehearse it" to remind the student of a specific strategy may be seen as less critical to a student because the instructor does not have to say the particular student's name. Throughout this book, suggestions for the short, telegraphic spoken reminders are printed in quotation marks after the title of each specific strategy. In this way, everyone in the group who is listening can benefit from the reminder.

With practice and reminders, using the strategy will become automatic. The students' independent awareness of when it might be appropriate to use the strategy will increase. Once the students have mastered how and when to use the new strategy, they can proceed successfully with the task at hand. With repeated self-choice, or independent application of a specific strategy, students may permanently add this new skill to their repertoire. They can then be ready to learn a new or more complex strategy in order to continue improving their learning.

In summary, the sequential steps, or recipe, for successfully instructing a student in the use of a strategy are:

1. Model the strategy for the student.

2. Have student perform the strategy with assistance.

3. Remind the student when the strategy could be used.

4. Praise the student every time the strategy is used.

5. Provide practice opportunities to use the strategy.

6. Encourage the student's self-choice to use the strategy.

7. Help the student master the strategy.

8. Select a new strategy.

How Do We Use the Strategy Sections of This Book?

The strategies are clustered into the three "brain" skill areas of learning. These mental skills are basic neurological processes that the brain must perform in the process of learning. To learn, we must be able to:

- Pay attention to the delivery of instruction.

- Have a memory of the information.

- Organize the information so we can use it in tasks.

To be able to learn effectively in different situations, students can apply additional techniques—known as strategies—to maximize or enhance their attention, memory, and organization. However, most struggling students need to learn strategies to compensate for specific weaknesses in one or more of these "brain" skills. Without a compensatory strategy to overcome their weakness, learning becomes increasingly difficult over the course of their school years, because they cannot pay attention, remember, or get organized.

A section is dedicated to each of the three brain processes: Section 2 discusses attention, Section 3 is devoted to memory, and Section 4 focuses on organization. Each section begins with a general description of what is involved in that particular area of learning. This information will prove invaluable because it provides a general definition and description that is written in everyday language.

Once you have read two or three strategies, you will become familiar with the book's overall format. Each strategy segment of the book contains a general description of the strategy, with a specific student example, and a complete description of how to teach the strategy to the student. Memory strategies include a recipe for step-by-step presentation of the information to the student. Organization strategies include essential background information on the educational reasoning for selecting a specific strategy.

At the beginning of the narrative for each strategy is a description of a specific student's frustrated behavior that can be overcome by using that strategy. You may want to read all the short behavior descriptions first, especially if you have a particular student in mind. Reading the behavior descriptions helps teachers and parents to recognize their own students' behaviors. That "ah ha—sounds like Tommy" feeling clearly helps the instructor recognize the strategy that might be the exact one needed for a specific student.

In addition, by reading all the behavioral descriptions first, you may gain an overall sense of the variety of strategies included in the sections. As a result, you will gain a better understanding of how to separate attention problems from memory problems, etc. As instructors, we must know the actual root of the problem in order to know where we should begin. After previewing, instructors will have a better understanding about which of the choices might be the most effective starting point for their students.

Section Two

Attention-Enhancing Strategies

· · · · · · · · · · · · · · · · · · ·

What Does It Mean to "Pay Attention"?

Attention is generally defined as the ability to focus one's mind on an object, sense, emotion, or thought. Attention precedes all learning. Without it, there is little—or at least limited—learning because there is nothing to remember in moments of distraction. When attention is not constant, or when it demands a great deal of concentration, confusion often results. In addition, if a student has trouble "screening out" nearby sounds and sights or internal thoughts, he or she most likely will be unable to maintain attention on the instruction. Although it may not be deliberate, the student's brain is "selecting" to attend to a stimulus other than the one he or she needs to be focused on. Thus, before we can expect the student to attend to our instruction, we may first need to change the environment in which she or he is working.

Paying attention is much more than merely appearing to be ready to listen to or look at something. Good attention is the ability to remain at attention, or have sustained attention, throughout a task. To complicate the process further, we can have good attention when we listen, but poor attention when we look at things (or vice versa). The details in listening or looking are very important for mastery of new knowledge. Often, a student is better at one kind of attention than the other. Adults are no different from young students in that they sometimes have to help themselves pay attention. To do this, adults will frequently develop special methods that they employ to focus their attention. For example, do you find that repeating someone's words or whispering under your breath helps increase your understanding? Or do you find it helpful to write down things as you listen to something new? These are just a few of the particular methods that help to focus one's attention.

Unfortunately, many children do not know how to help themselves pay attention in particular instances because they have not yet recognized their personal style of attending. So, as instructors, one of our first responsibilities is to ensure that students can begin to attend at the moment instruction commences and remain at attention throughout the task. We also need to help students understand when they must do additional things to boost their attention and concentration. To accomplish this, we must be aware of when it is difficult or easy for them to attend. Through the observation of their behaviors while learning, we can determine what distracts their attention, when and how they become distracted, and what kinds of activities hold their attention for longer periods of time.

By noting on an ongoing basis what distracts a certain student and what he or she finds difficult to attend to, we can determine the areas of weak attention and select the strategies that will compensate for them. The use of a compensatory strategy will initially require reminders and praise to reinforce its value. But in time, with encouragement and practice, the student will learn to self-initiate the use of a strategy. By experiencing the positive results of increased attention, the student will feel more successful and confident.

How Are the Attention Strategies Organized?

The strategies in this section are specifically designed to improve a student's attention. They are purposely ordered by the complexity of the skill they are addressing. The first strategies involve the most basic visual skill—*scanning* or moving one's eyes consistently from left-to-right—in an analysis of pictures, letter symbols, word forms, and, finally, printed rows of reading text. Next, strategies are provided for scanning entire surfaces from top to bottom, so as to see all that is present. Then strategies that improve analysis of printed paper tasks are explored. These suggestions will increase accuracy on worksheet-like school tasks that attempt to test students' skills. The problem here, however, could be that the student might be frustrated by the layout of the task rather than not having the skills that are required to complete it successfully. Finally, the last items provide varied strategies for self-checking work to improve accuracy monitoring. Each student will have a preference because the self-checking strategies are based on various sensory inputs.

● Strategy 2-1: Consistent Left-to-Right Scanning

"left to right"

Observed Behavior

Tommy reads rapidly, but often reads words backward. In spelling, he misses words and writes similar ones without noticing his error. For example, instead of "stop," he writes "spot." When he writes answers to addition problems, he often reverses the order of the digits; instead of "21," he writes "12."

In order to make sense, the world of print in the English language must be scanned from left to right. This can be demonstrated by showing the students that the word "cat," read backward becomes "tac"; "was" becomes "saw." The word "was" must be seen in order as w-a-s to be recognized and make sense in a sentence. Numbers must also be scanned from left to right. The number "21" read backward is "12." All multidigit numbers are spoken in the left-to-right order that matches the order in which they are printed. For example, "forty-one" is written in spoken order with the "four" written first followed by the "one," hence "41." The exceptions, of course, are the "teen" numbers. For example, "fourteen" is not written in the spoken order "4" "teen."

To correct this behavior, students must learn to automatically start looking at the print on the left-hand side of tasks and move toward the right. How do we teach students to read and write in a left-to-right progression?

Strategies and Tools to Improve the Student's Performance

1. Remember which direction is left, so we know where to start. Consistent eye movement—scanning from left to right—can be encouraged by using visible arrow and circle markers. The markers can be color-coded with green in the arrow for "go that way" and red in the circle for "stop."

You may wish to use the following illustration to demonstrate the use of green and red color-coded markers on a printed page. It would also be appropriate to display the illustration as a CUE CARD on the students' desks or on the bulletin board to remind students to use the strategy.

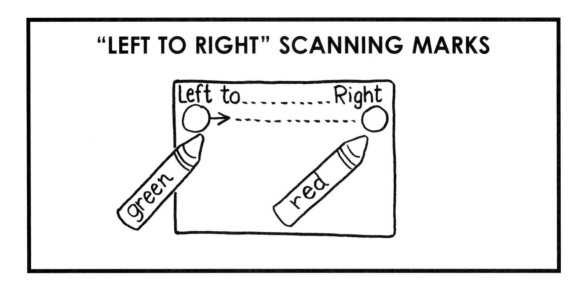

2. Practice concrete direction by drawing lines from left to right. Before students actually draw lines, we can teach them to imagine that their eyes work like a car on a printed page. The car starts along the left-hand side of the page as if sitting at a stoplight waiting for the light to turn from red to green. When the light does turn to green, the car does not go backward. Rather, the car moves forward, going toward the right. At the end of the road, it stops at the red light and then drives around to the next line, or road. (It still does not go backward.)

Use the sample task below to model left to right scanning. Dotted lines show that the car is going from left to right to reach its final destination to purchase an ice cream cone, a kite, a pet, whatever. Children should draw a line from left to right, showing the direction that the car will go to reach its destination. Before they begin the worksheet, have the students color in the direction marks along the right and left margins. The arrow markers on the left should be colored green. The circle markers on the right should be colored red. This activity will build stronger memory for left-to-right progression by activating the student's tactile-kinesthetic learning. A full-page worksheet for this activity is available at the end of this strategy section.

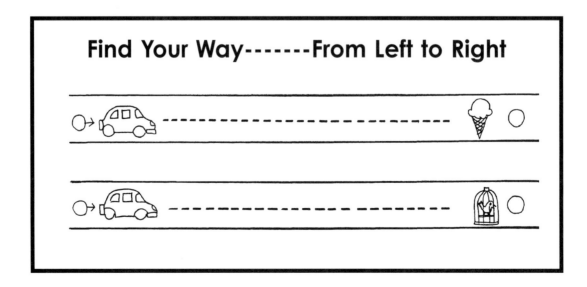

To reinforce the left-to-right concept, students could act it out by using toy cars to drive along a "print" road. At the end of the road, they would drive in a half-circle motion back to the start of the next "print" road. Once the student has learned the strategy for using green markers on print roads, green arrow markers should be placed at the top left corner of all papers and on the top left-hand corner of the students' desks. The red-light circle should be placed on the right side to indicate the need to "drive" their eyes back around to the green light and start over again on the left side.

3. Use students' hands for left and right when direction markers are not available. The human left hand, when outstretched, makes a capital "L" for "Left." It's unexplainable, but most students do not become confused by the reversed "L" shape on the right hand. They know which one is the real letter "L." You may wish to reproduce the following illustration to demonstrate how to find left-to-right directionality by using your hands. Note that the following illustration contains the left direction arrow, which should be colored green. The right circle marker for stop should be colored red.

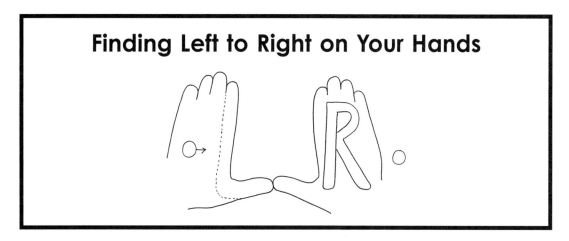

Finding Left to Right on Your Hands

4. Remind students that when their thumb tips touch and their hands are flat on the table, their hands will frame a paper task. The "L" hand will be on the left side of the page. That shows the students where the scanning must start. You may wish to reproduce the following illustration and display it so students will see the picture and remember the strategy.

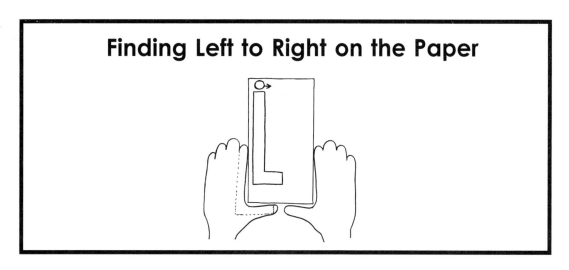

Finding Left to Right on the Paper

5. Practice left-to-right scanning with younger students by having them find pictures in left-to-right order. To prevent students from peeking down a page, it is suggested that you use another piece of paper or cardboard strip to cover everything below the row on which they are working. Direct the task by saying, "When your eyes are ready to move down to the next green-light go marker, I'll say 'ready, go.' Then we'll mark the pictures in the next row." This activity should not be done independently. Without specific direction and teacher observation, the student could successfully complete it using right-to-left scanning, which would reinforce "backward" scanning.

Following is a sample picture-scanning task. Additional full-page worksheets are included at the end of this strategy section.

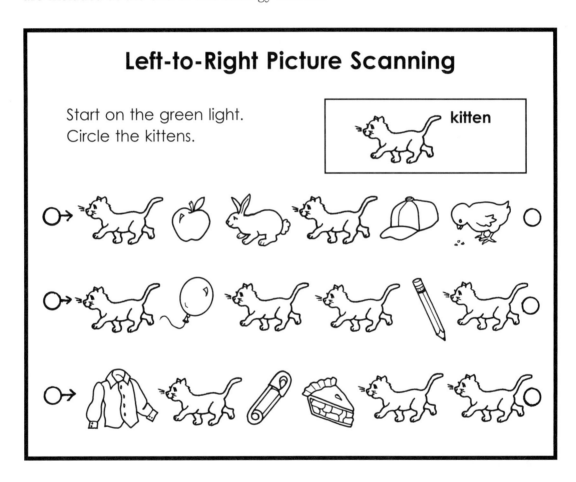

6. Create picture-scanning tasks with a set of picture stamps and an ink pad. Select one item and label the task at the top with the specific picture to be found while scanning. Alternate the stamps, randomly repeating the selected item, through six to eight rows.

Worksheets

Consistent Left-to-Right Scanning

- Find Your Way--------From Left to Right
- Circle the Kittens
- Put a Line Under the Monkeys
- Put an X on the Birds

Find Your Way------From Left to Right

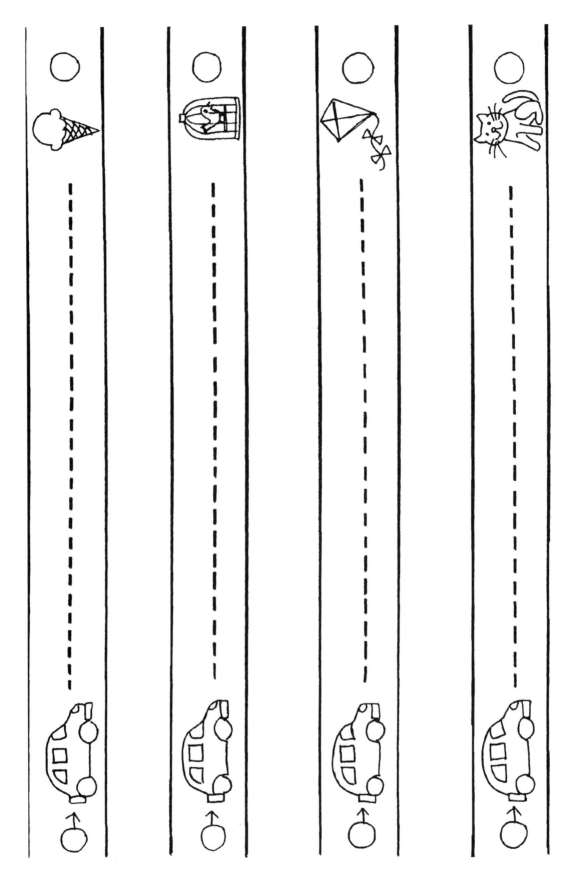

Name_____ Date_____

Circle the kittens.

 **kitten**

Put a line under the monkeys.

 **monkey**

 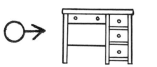   

Name_____ Date_____

Put an **X** on the birds.

 bird

 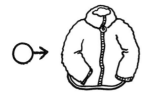

◆ Strategy 2-2: Left-to-Right Scanning of Letters

"scan it . . . letters"

Observed Behavior

Roberto is having difficulty recognizing and writing a majority of the lowercase letters. He pauses before writing each letter on his paper because he does not know where to start the letter "shape" or order the parts to create the whole letter. His teacher has helped him trace and practice each letter of the alphabet on a separate sheet of paper to improve his hand movements.

Although Roberto has practiced writing his letters, he still does not understand how to compare the letter symbols, analyze the letter parts, or put the parts in left-to-right order. If the student does not know how to examine the parts of letter symbols, they can be very confusing. Letter parts are called *strokes*. Many letters have the same strokes, but they are in a different order or position. As instructors we can demonstrate how to examine lowercase letters by using the directional left-to-right arrow strategy or "green-light go" to identify the order of the strokes in letters.

Strategies and Tools to Improve the Student's Performance

Students may need to review the previously described left-to-right strategy, which was used with picture scanning, to recognize its relevance to letters. The arrow should be explained—in student language—as the place where our eyes must start looking and then move forward in a left-to-right direction to be able to see the correct order in which the parts are used to make letters. Students should be encouraged to draw their own letter arrows and color them green. The motor movements of drawing and coloring increase the students' mastery of left-to-right letter analysis.

Although the directional left-to-right arrow is successful in helping most students master the identification of lowercase letters, some students remain confused. The lowercase letters are particularly difficult because there are so many different kinds of strokes. The basic "strokes" used for lowercase letters are the following: *tall lines, short lines, slanted lines, horizontal lines, hook lines, circle shapes, closed at top curves, open at top curves,* and *dots on letters.* Young students could be encouraged to use toy cars to "drive" across letters in a left-to-right direction. Each letter should be introduced with a directional arrow preceding it. As students move their car in a left-to-right direction across the letter, ask them to tell you which part of the letter is "bumped" first.

1. Teach students to correctly scan the order of individual strokes used in letters. The order of letter parts can be better interpreted by drawing a direction marker on the left side of the letter or by using a green marker as a cue to start on the left and go toward the right. This illustration can be used as a CUE CARD reminder to help students remember to use the "scan it . . . letters" strategy.

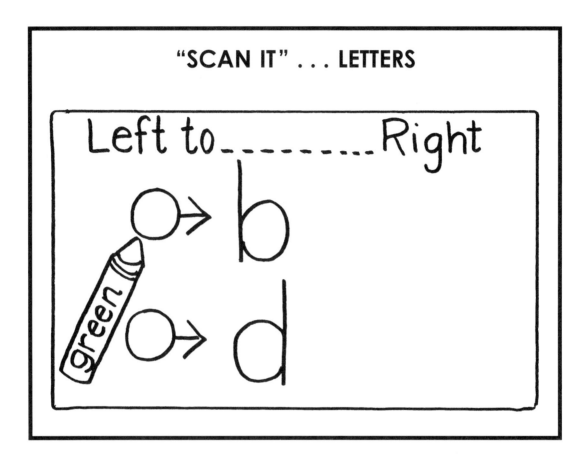

Students who are frustrated with visual analysis of small details must also be shown that letters can vary by their intended positions on a line. The students must be able to determine where the letters should be "standing" in relation to the "ground." However, the "ground line," on which each letter must stand in a specific position, is not always marked on the initial tasks used in letter instruction. Many of the classroom alphabet charts and letter strips do not place letters on a line. Without a visible ground line, the student must be able to estimate that some letters appear to be taller or seem to "hang down" on these classroom aids.

The student who is struggling with letter discrimination will likely remain confused about many similar letters until he or she receives instruction about the importance of the "ground line." For example, wouldn't it be helpful for the student to learn that the lowercase letters "f" and "j" both have a "hook line," but the "f" hook is above the ground as compared to the "j" which has a hook that hangs down below the ground line? Therefore, above and beyond the ability to analyze letter differences by noting the left-to-right order of "strokes" and identifying the various "strokes" that can be included in letter symbols, the student must also recognize where the letters should stand in relation to the "ground line." Some struggling students need practice in all three variables to master the lowercase letters.

2. Practice tasks to find specific "strokes" in letters that are placed on lines. Students who are encountering difficulty with letter mastery should have the opportunity to scan the alphabet to find these basic "strokes" so they can compare differences. Drills for inspecting the parts of letters of the alphabet can improve students' ability to automatically recognize the letter forms. Tasks that include all the letters of the alphabet placed on lines improve students' ability to compare and contrast letters, thereby improving their analysis skills. Repeated practice is necessary for mastery.

The following sample task asks the student to trace only the part of each letter that would be "bumped" first by the car. This is a left-to-right letter-scanning task. Make sure the students color the arrow markers on the left green and the circle markers red.

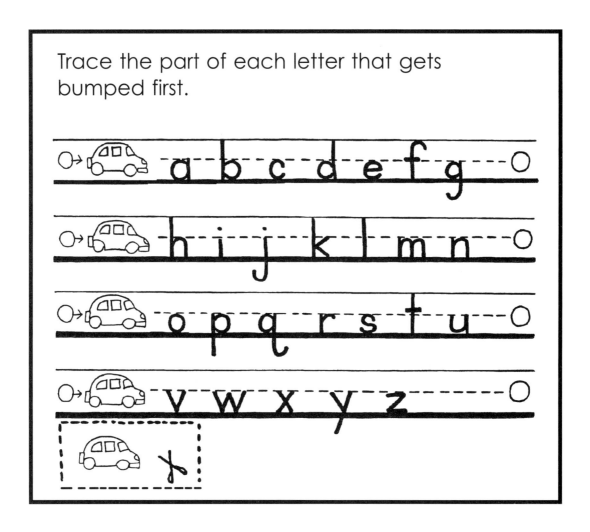

A copy of the worksheet without a direction line appears at the end of this strategy section. You may wish to add directions as needed depending on the letter part you want the student to locate in the task. Some suggestions for directions include the following:

- Trace all the letters that have circle parts.
- Trace all the letters that have circle parts that come first.
- Trace all the letters that have tall stick parts.
- Trace all the letters that have tall stick parts that come first.
- Trace all the letters that have curves that are closed at the top.
- Trace all the letters that have "hang down" parts.
- Trace all the letters that have "hooks."
- Trace all the letters that have dots.
- Trace all the letters that have slanted lines.

Worksheet

Scanning Parts of Letters in the Alphabet

Note:

- This worksheet is intentionally untitled to allow you to vary the task and add your own instructions.

- The car cut-out illustration at the bottom of the page can be removed, copied, and laminated to make a permanent set of cars for students to use when they are scanning letters.

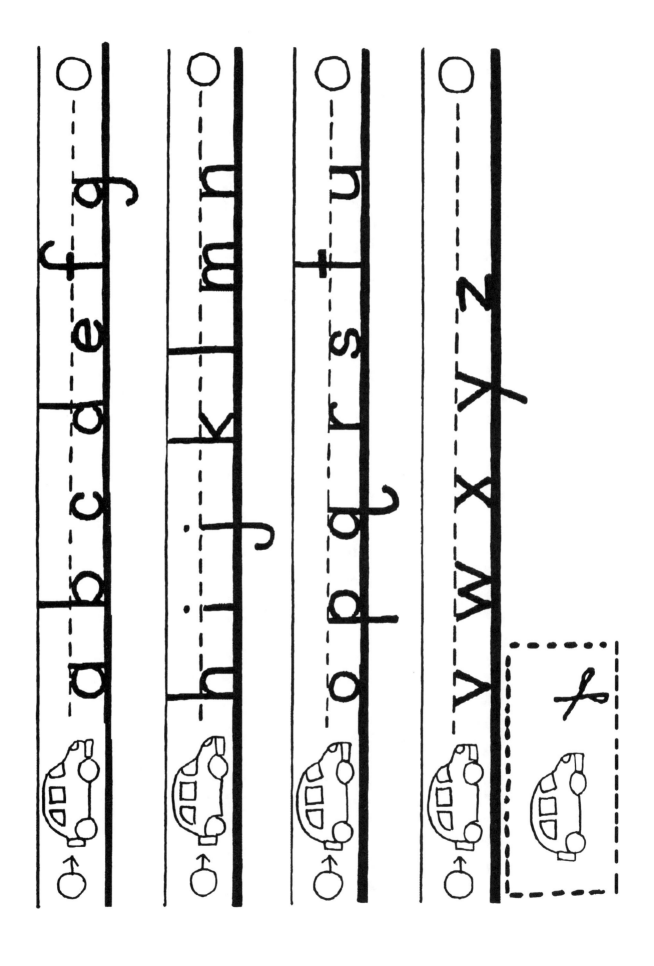

◆» Strategy 2-3: Pictographs for Remembering Difficult Letters "use the letter pictures"

Observed Behavior

*Amy becomes very confused when she tries to read or write words containing the letters **b**, **d**, **p**, and **q**. She looks around the room for a model of the letters to check to see if she is writing them correctly. When she tries to read these letters inside words, she is not sure which one is which, even with help from the model. She has to look so carefully at each letter inside a word that she loses concentration and makes mistakes.*

Amy has learned to correctly identify a majority of the letter symbols by using the left-to-right directional marker strategy; however, she continues to be frustrated with specific letters. The letters **b**, **d**, **p**, and **q** are particularly difficult to differentiate for students who have problems with interpreting small visual details. These letters are often referred to as *reversals* (**b/d**, **p/q**) because they are written in the reverse order of another similar letter. The **b** and **d** pair and the **p** and **q** pair are mirror images of each other. Other letters that flip over from top to bottom (**u/n**, **W/M**) are also confusing. These letters are referred to as *inversions* or *rotations* because they move to a different position on the line.

Strategies and Tools to Improve the Student's Performance

All students who have difficulty with these letters benefit from instruction on how to use a left-to-right direction marker to improve their ability to accurately scan them in the correct order. However, for students like Amy, who continue to be confused, instructors need to explore the use of a strategy that employs a different sensory mode. Amy may benefit from strategies that employ meaningful visual information.

Would her analysis skills for these letters improve if she had a picture that matched each difficult letter shape? Would her memory for the pictures be increased if we encouraged her to trace or draw the pictures? Although she most likely will need to continue to use the left-to-right directional marker, Amy might improve her recall of the difficult letters by focusing on her visual memory for pictures and her motor memory for drawing.

1. Draw pictures to improve recall of reversed letters (b, d, p, q). Pictographs can be used to help students with the letters that reverse or appear as mirror images of each other. The drawings exactly match the shapes of these letters to improve the students' memory for determining which letter is which. With the use of meaningful drawings, we activate a student's visual picture memory. Please note each letter is preceded with the left-to-right direction marker. The illustrations can be reproduced individually and used as CUE CARDS to be placed across the student's desk; or they can be reproduced as a group and displayed on a bulletin board as a reminder for students. At the end of this strategy section, instructors will find a full-page worksheet for each reversible letter.

"Use the Letter Pictures"

2. Discuss each of the reversible letters (b, d, p, q). Students need to discuss each letter, so they can recognize *likenesses* and *differences* in the similar letter pictures.

Say: "The **b** looks like a bumblebee with its stinger coming first."

You might point out that the stinger points upward because the bee would fly upward.

Say: "The **p** looks like a pencil with the long side of the pencil coming first."

You might point out that the pencil points downward for writing on the paper.

Say: "The **d** looks like a dog named Dee Dee."

You might point out that the dog's nose, or circle part, comes first. This shows that it is a "d."

Say: "The **q**, which always has a **u** with it, looks like a queen."

You might point out that the picture of the queen contains both letters, which are used to create the queen's eyes and nose. If the **q** were reversed to a **p**, it would look like **pu** and that makes a face without a nose line between the eyes.

3. Draw pictures to improve recall of easily inverted letters (n, u, h, r, M, W). These letters can be seen as inverted, or upside down. Picture drawings that match the actual shape of these letters improve the student's ability to recognize which one is which. By encouraging students to draw or trace the pictures, we can activate their visual picture memory. Be sure to add the direction arrow in front of each letter/picture. At the end of this strategy section, instructors will find a full-page worksheet for each inverted letter.

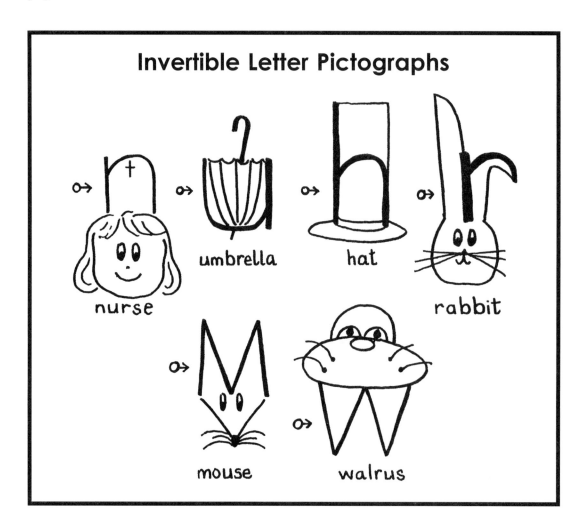

Invertible Letter Pictographs

nurse   umbrella   hat   rabbit

mouse   walrus

4. Discuss each of the inverted letters (u, n, h, r, M, W). Students need to discuss each letter picture, as well as compare similar letter pictures.

Say: "The **n** looks like a nurse with her cap."

You might point out that the curve is closed at the top.

Say: "The **h** looks like a Mr. Lincoln hat."

You might point out that it has a beginning tall stick and a closed top-curve.

Say: "The **u** looks like an umbrella."

You might point out that the curve is open at the top this time. Students might giggle, thinking of an upside-down umbrella turning into a swimming pool that fills with rain.

Say: "The **r** looks like a rabbit."

You might point out that one ear is flopped over with a half-curve.

Say: "The **M** looks like a mouse."

You might point out that the points stick up like ears.

Say: "The **W** looks like a walrus."

You might point out that the points go downward for the walrus's tusks.

5. Perform drills for scanning all the difficult letters in mixed sets of similar letters. Letters that are easily confused often require additional practice. To improve the accurate identification of a specific letter in a mixed set of similar letters, all students benefit from having the pictograph within view. The following sample task is for a specific letter. At the end of this strategy section, you will find full-size pages for all the letter-scan tasks.

Scanning for Letter d

The letter **d** should have a circle first and a stick last.
If you draw a picture around the **d**, it becomes a dog.

Move your eyes from left to right.
Circle the **d** letters in each row.

O→b d p p d b d p q q b d p q b O

O→p p b d d b b p d q p b d p q O

O→q p d b b q p d b b d q p d p O

Worksheets

Letter Reversal Drawings

- Draw the bee.
- Draw the pencil.
- Draw Dee Dee dog.
- Draw the queen.

Draw the bee.

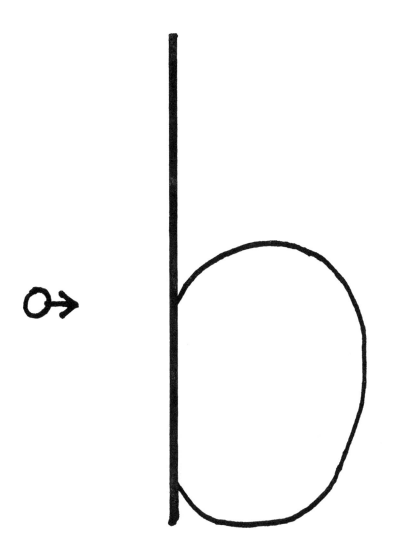

Can you see the o→ will bump into the stinger-stick **FIRST**?

Draw the pencil.

p

o→

Can you see the o→ will bump
into the stick part FIRST?

Draw Dee Dee dog.

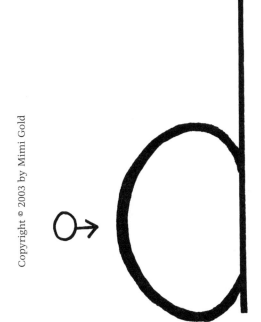

Can you see the o→ will bump into Dee Dee's nose FIRST?

Draw the queen.

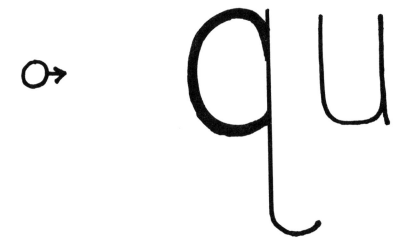

Can you see the o→ will bump the
queen's eye first and then her nose?
The nose is in the middle of her face!

Worksheets

Inverted Letter Drawings

- Draw the umbrella.
- Draw the nurse.
- Draw the tall hat.
- Draw the rabbit.
- Draw the mice.
- Draw the walrus.

Note: In each worksheet that follows, children should color the arrows in the left-hand margin green.

  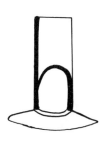 

Draw the umbrella.

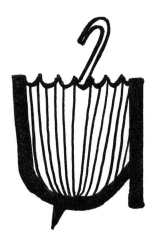

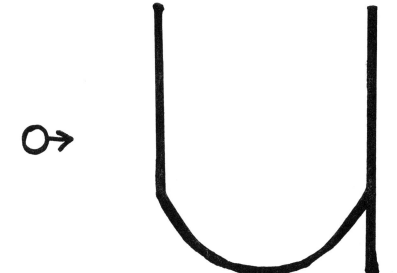

Draw the nurse.

Draw the tall hat.

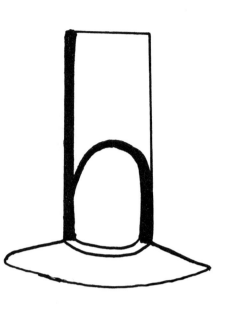

Name_____ Date_____

Draw the rabbit.

Draw the mice.

 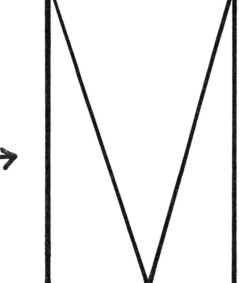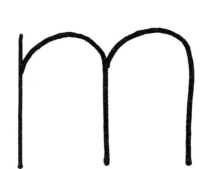

Draw the walrus.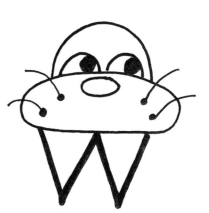

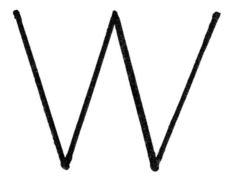

Worksheets

Scanning for Specific Letters with Mixed Sets

- Scanning for Letter **b**
- Scanning for Letter **p**
- Scanning for Letter **d**
- Scanning for Letter **q**
- Scanning for Letter **u**
- Scanning for Letter **n**
- Scanning for Letter **h**
- Scanning for Letter r
- Scanning for Letter **m**
- Scanning for Letter **M**
- Scanning for Letter **W**

Scanning for Letter b

The letter **b** should have a stick first and a circle last.
If you draw a picture around the **b**, it becomes a bee.
Remember, bees fly upward, so his stinger-stick points up.

Move your eyes from left to right.
Circle the **b** letters in each row.

O→b d p p d b d p q q b d p q b O

O→p p b d d b b p q q p b d p q O

O→q p d b b q p p b b d q p d p O

O→b q q b d d p p d b q b p p q O

O→p p q b d d b q p p b q b q p O

O→q b d d d q p p q d b b q d b p O

Scanning for Letter p

The letter **p** should have a stick first and a circle last.
If you draw a picture around the **p**, it becomes a pencil.
Remember, a pencil points down, so we can write on paper.

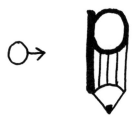

Move your eyes from left to right.
Circle the **p** letters in each row.

O→b d p d d b q p q q p d p q b O

O→p q b d d p b p d q q b d p q O

O→q p d b b q p d p b d q p d p O

O→b d q p d d b p d p q b p d q O

O→p d q b d d b q p p b q d q p O

O→q b p b q p d d q d p b q d b p O

Scanning for Letter d

The letter **d** should have a circle first and a stick last.
If you draw a picture around the **d**, it becomes a dog.

Move your eyes from left to right.
Circle the **d** letters in each row.

○→b d p p d b d p q q b d p q b ○

○→p p b d d b b p d q p b d p q ○

○→q p d b b q p d b b d q p d p ○

○→b d q b d d p p d b q b p p q ○

○→p d q b d d b q p p b q d q p ○

○→q b d b q p d d q d b b q d b p ○

Scanning for Letter q

The letter **q** should have a circle first and a stick last.
If you draw a picture around the **q**, it becomes a queen.

Move your eyes from left to right.
Circle the **q** letters in each row.

O→ b q p d d b q p q b p d p q b O

O→ p q b d d p b p d q q b d p q O

O→ q p d b b q p d q b d q p d p O

O→ b d q p d q b p d p q b p d q O

O→ p d q b d d b q p p b q d q p O

O→ q b p b b q p d q d p b q d b p O

Scanning for Letter u

The letter **u** should have a down-curve first and stick last.
If you draw a picture around the **u**, it becomes an umbrella.

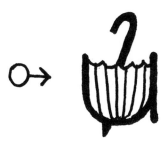

Move your eyes from left to right.
Circle the **u** letters in each row.

○→ n u m m h h u m n u h r r u n ○

○→ u m n h u r u u m n r r h n n ○

○→ h r n u u m n u h h r u n n r ○

○→ u n n m h u r u m n r u h n h ○

○→ n u m m h n u r h u n m n u r ○

○→ m m u n h u h r n u m u n m h ○

Scanning for Letter n

The letter **n** should have a stick first and an up-curve last.
If you draw a picture around the **n**, it becomes a nurse.

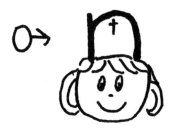

Move your eyes from left to right.
Circle the **n** letters in each row.

n u m m h h u m n u h n r u n

u m n h u r u u m n r r h n n

h r n u n m n u h h r u n u r

u n n m h u r u m n r u h n h

n u m m h n u r h u n m n u r

m m u n h u n r n u m u n m h

Scanning for Letter h

The letter **h** should have a stick first and an up-curve last.
If you draw a picture around the **h**, it becomes a hat.

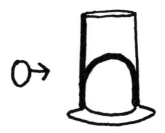

Move your eyes from left to right.
Circle the **h** letters in each row.

n u h m h r u h n u m h r u n

u h n h m r n h n r r h m n

h m n u n h n u h m r u m h r

u m h m h u r u h n r n m n h

n h m n h n m r h m n m h u r

h n u n h m n r n m h u n m h

Scanning for Letter r

The letter **r** should have a stick first and a small curve last.
If you draw a picture around the **r**, it becomes a rabbit.

Move your eyes from left to right.
Circle the **r** letters in each row.

○→ n r m m h r u m n u h r r u n ○

○→ r m n h u r u u m n r r h n n ○

○→ h r n u u r n u h h r u n n r ○

○→ u n r m h u r u m n r u h r h ○

○→ r u m m h n r r h u n m n u r ○

○→ m r u n h u h r n u m r r m h ○

Scanning for Letter m

The letter **m** should have two up-curves.
If you draw a picture around the **m**, it becomes a baby mouse.

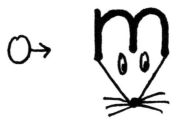

Move your eyes from left to right.
Circle the **m** letters in each row.

O→ n u m m h h u m n u m n r u n O

O→ u m n h m r n n m n r r h m n O

O→ h m n u n m n u h m r u m u r O

O→ u m n m h u r u m n r n m n h O

O→ n u m n h n m r h m n m n u r O

O→ m n u n h m n r n m m u n m h O

Scanning for Letter M

The letter **M** should have a stick first and two down-slants.
If you draw a picture around the **M**, it becomes a mouse with big ears.

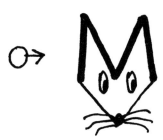

Move your eyes from left to right.
Circle the **M** letters in each row.

O→ M W W M W N M W N N W M W N O

O→ W W M N N W H M W N N M W M N O

O→ N N W M N W W M W N N M W M N O

O→ M N W W M M W W H N N M N W W O

O→ W W M N N M W W W M N N W M N O

O→ N N N M W M W W W M N N M W W N O

Scanning for Letter W

The letter **W** should have a tall down-slant first.
If you draw a picture around the **W**, it becomes a walrus.

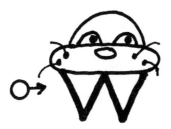

Move your eyes from left to right.
Circle the **W** letters in each row.

O→ M W N M W N M W N N N N M W N O

O→ W W M N N W H M H N N M W M N O

O→ N N W M N W W M N N N M W M N O

O→ M N W W M M W M H N N M N W M O

O→ W M M N N M W M W M N N W M N O

O→ N N W M W M M N W M N M N W N O

Strategy 2-4: Scanning of Words   "word scan"

Observed Behavior

When Yuri writes a word on the page, he always makes a spelling mistake in the middle of the word. The word will have the correct number of letters and often look similar, but it is not quite right. He knows it looks funny, but he can't figure out how to correct it.

Many students read words as shapes. It's as if they see a special box drawn around the outside of the word that matches its exact shape. This is called a word's configuration. The students do not actually see the specific order of letters inside the word, unless you draw their attention to it. Most of us, sooner or later, figure out words by using the logic of the sentence context; we are not often forced to look at the letters in the word. Often, we can figure out an unknown word by looking at the first letter alone. If we get really stuck, we can look inside the word at specific letters. However, non-scanners of letter order in words make mistakes in their analysis of the letters in the words. As a result, they often make incorrect word choices that interfere with their comprehension of the details in a reading passage and increase the number of errors in spelling and writing.

Strategies and Tools to Improve the Student's Performance

So, what can be done? As instructors, we can provide opportunities for finding parts of words that do not match in sets of similar words. Over the years, we have all been asked to look at three word choices and select the two that are identical. But identifying two words that are the same does not force us to look inside the word because we can identify the two words that have the same shape or configuration. Instead, we must provide word sets that are nearly identical with the exception of one or two letters. If students are required to search for the incorrect letters in the non-matching word, they will have to look inside the word. We will need to teach students techniques for cross-checking so they can carefully and accurately inspect the words. We also need to teach students to say the names of the letters aloud, so they know what letters they actually see. Finally, we need to teach them to scan for chunks or pieces of each word, in order to break the word into more manageable parts. Practice in any form can increase students' use of scanning to improve accuracy.

1. Teach simple word scanning to young readers. The following sample task can be used to introduce simple word scanning to *beginning* readers. At the end of this strategy section is a series of worksheets that provides the opportunity for a young reader to practice "looking inside" words, noting the actual order of letters that are inside a word. As an instructor, you can easily create your own similar tasks by using currently available worksheets to help students improve their ability to discriminate visually. These tasks normally have a three-column format in which the student must circle the two words that are the same. To ensure that students check the letters inside each word, an additional instruction should be added: "Cross out the letter or letters in the word that does not match."

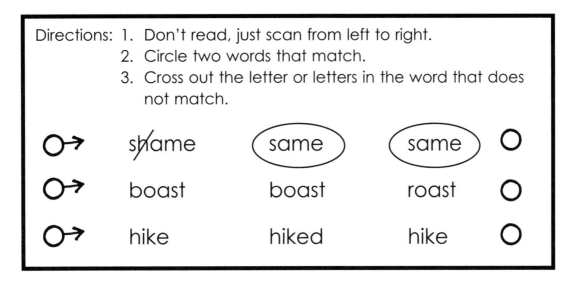

2. Teach complex word scanning for more advanced students. The following sample task is for older students and/or *more advanced* readers. It is also one of a series of worksheets that provides the opportunity for a fluent reader to practice "looking inside" words to note the actual order of letters that are within a word. You can create your own word-scanning sheets by using existing materials, but you must add the additional instruction, "Cross out the EXTRA letter or letters in the word that does not match."

Name_____ Date_____ Score =_____ out of 10

Complex Word Scanning
Letter Additions

Directions: 1. Don't read, just scan from left to right.
2. Circle two words that match.
3. Cross out the EXTRA letter or letters in the word that does not match.

⊙→ (spit)   (spit)   split   ○

⊙→ gown   grown   gown   ○

⊙→ stated   stated   started   ○

Worksheets

Simple Word Scanning for Younger Students

- Word Scanning 1
- Word Scanning 2
- Word Scanning 3
- Word Scanning 4
- Word Scanning 5
- Word Scanning 6

Simple Word Scanning 1

Directions: 1. Don't read, just scan from left to right.
2. Circle two words that match.
3. Cross out the letter or letters in the word that does not match.

O→	~~s~~hame	(same)	(same)	O
O→	boast	boast	roast	O
O→	hike	hiked	hike	O
O→	band	band	bang	O
O→	return	turn	turn	O
O→	buck	puck	buck	O
O→	load	load	loading	O
O→	light	lighter	light	O
O→	itch	itches	itch	O
O→	cooker	cooker	cook	O
O→	seen	unseen	unseen	O

Simple Word Scanning 2

Directions: 1. Don't read, just scan from left to right.
2. Circle two words that match.
3. Cross out the letter or letters in the word that does not match.

⊙→	(see)	(see)	se~~t~~	○
⊙→	beans	bean	bean	○
⊙→	clock	click	clock	○
⊙→	waiting	wait	wait	○
⊙→	soak	sick	soak	○
⊙→	main	main	chain	○
⊙→	kick	king	kick	○
⊙→	path	bath	bath	○
⊙→	quest	request	quest	○
⊙→	cold	gold	gold	○
⊙→	tack	talk	tack	○

Simple Word Scanning 3

Directions: 1. Don't read, just scan from left to right.
2. Circle two words that match.
3. Cross out the letter or letters in the word that does not match.

(land)	lane	(land)
hug	hug	bun
pack	pack	back
undo	do	do
shake	snake	snake
bath	bang	bang
peat	peat	beat
run	run	runs
belt	unbelt	belt
clock	clink	clink
match	matches	match

Simple Word Scanning 4

Directions: 1. Don't read, just scan from left to right.
2. Circle two words that match.
3. Cross out the letter or letters in the word that does not match.

O→	(do)	(do)	~~un~~do	O
O→	sand	band	sand	O
O→	blink	blank	blink	O
O→	paint	paint	saint	O
O→	return	return	turn	O
O→	house	house	horse	O
O→	tour	detour	tour	O
O→	hope	home	hope	O
O→	cart	cart	card	O
O→	sleep	sleeping	sleep	O
O→	jumpy	jumpy	jump	O

Simple Word Scanning 5

Directions: 1. Don't read, just scan from left to right.
2. Circle two words that match.
3. Cross out the letter or letters in the word that does not match.

(wish)	(wish)	~~f~~ish	
swim	grim	swim	
vest	vest	west	
grab	grip	grab	
rush	rush	gush	
crutch	crunch	crunch	
clan	clap	clan	
went	went	wing	
tine	time	time	
sled	sled	slid	
when	then	when	

Simple Word Scanning 6

Directions: 1. Don't read, just scan from left to right.
2. Circle two words that match.
3. Cross out the letter or letters in the word that does not match.

⟶	(make)	(make)	ma~~k~~e	◯
⟶	boat	boat	boar	◯
⟶	yell	retell	yell	◯
⟶	soap	soak	soap	◯
⟶	lock	block	block	◯
⟶	poor	poorer	poor	◯
⟶	long	long	gong	◯
⟶	camper	camper	camp	◯
⟶	look	loot	look	◯
⟶	clock	click	click	◯
⟶	hide	hide	hire	◯

Worksheets

Complex Word Scanning for Advanced Students

- Word Scanning 1: Prefix and Suffix Additions
- Word Scanning 2: Letter Additions
- Word Scanning 3: Prefix and Suffix Omissions
- Word Scanning 4: Substitutions
- Word Scanning 5: Mixed Additions and Omissions
- Word Scanning 6: Shifts or "Switching Places"

Complex Word Scanning 1:
Prefix and Suffix Additions

Directions: 1. <u>Don't</u> read, just scan from left to right.
2. Circle the two words that match.
3. Cross out the EXTRA letter or letters in the word that does not match.

O→ (just)	(just)	~~un~~just O
O→ help	helpless	help O
O→ jump	jumper	jump O
O→ become	come	come O
O→ branch	branches	branch O
O→ test	test	retest O
O→ hilltop	hilly	hilly O
O→ delight	light	light O
O→ round	roundest	round O
O→ open	openly	open O

Complex Word Scanning 2:
Letter Additions

Directions: 1. <u>Don't</u> read, just scan from left to right.
2. Circle the two words that match.
3. Cross out the EXTRA letter or letters in the word that does not match.

⊙→	(spit)	(spit)	spl̸it	○
⊙→	gown	grown	gown	○
⊙→	stated	stated	started	○
⊙→	clap	clap	clamp	○
⊙→	rings	springs	rings	○
⊙→	sooner	schooner	sooner	○
⊙→	ice	ice	splice	○
⊙→	band	bandage	band	○
⊙→	amps	amps	stamps	○
⊙→	painter	pain	pain	○

Complex Word Scanning 3:
Prefix and Suffix Omissions

Directions: 1. <u>Don't</u> read, just scan from left to right.
2. Circle the two words that match.
3. Make slashes (/) where letters have been SKIPPED.

O→ (unfair)   (unfair)   //fair   O

O→ shapeless   shape   shapeless   O

O→ climber   climber   climb   O

O→ hold   behold   behold   O

O→ crunches   crunch   crunches   O

O→ resale   sale   resale   O

O→ defend   fend   defend   O

O→ sick   sickness   sickness   O

O→ steep   steepest   steepest   O

O→ quickly   quickly   quick   O

Complex Word Scanning 4:
Substitutions

Directions: 1. <u>Don't</u> read, just scan from left to right.
2. Circle the two words that match.
3. Make slashes (/) where letters have been SKIPPED.

ba/ker	(banker)	(banker)
sparing	sparkling	sparing
herd	heard	heard
spears	ears	spears
clams	clamps	clamps
ringy	springy	springy
word	world	world
camped	cramped	cramped
basking	baking	basking
splice	splice	lice

Complex Word Scanning 5:
Mixed Additions and Omissions

Directions: 1. <u>Don't</u> read, just scan from left to right.
2. Circle the two words that match.
3. In the wrong word, check the beginning of the word, the end, and the middle.
4. Make slashes (/) where the letter or letters are EXTRA or SKIPPED.

O→ (baker)	ba/nker	(baker) O
O→ fair	unfair	unfair O
O→ split	split	spit O
O→ just	just	unjust O
O→ sparing	sparing	sparkling O
O→ shapeless	shape	shapeless O
O→ gown	grown	gown O
O→ help	helpful	help O
O→ herd	heard	heard O
O→ climber	climber	climb O

Complex Word Scanning 6:
Shifts or "Switching Places"

Directions: 1. <u>Don't</u> read, just scan from left to right.
2. Circle the two words that match.
3. Find the letters that SWITCHED PLACES in the wrong word.
4. Make a "flipper" mark (⌒) above the switched letters.

O→ (notes)	tones	(notes) O
O→ pears	spear	pears O
O→ steel	steel	sleet O
O→ smile	miles	smile O
O→ tips	tips	spit O
O→ tags	stag	stag O
O→ spot	spot	stop O
O→ drive	diver	diver O
O→ tales	stale	tales O

◖➤ Strategy 2-5: Tracking Rows of Print "track it"

Observed Behavior

Every time Ann reads a story out loud, she gets lost moving from one line of print to the next. Often, words from nearby lines of print pop into the sentence she is reading. Sometimes she doesn't even notice that her reading is not making sense.

Reading for meaning demands that we read rows of print in their correct order from left to right and top to bottom down the page. Yet, many struggling students have difficulty with this visual skill. Often, they cannot keep their eyes on the line of print they are reading because their eyes are drawn upward (*upward gaze*) to the line above or downward (*downward gaze*) to the line below. They can also encounter difficulty moving from the end of one line of print to the beginning of the next row of print (*shifting gaze*) for continued reading. The upward, downward, or shifting gaze can result in confusion for the student and a lack of understanding of the text the student has read.

Strategies and Tools to Improve the Student's Performance

Many teachers discourage students from using their fingers to track along the lines of print because they believe it can disrupt the flow of reading. Although this is true for some students, *finger tracking* may be essential for Ann who is unable to stay on the line of print without using her finger to guide her eyes.

Experiment with different styles of finger tracking to determine the student's personal choice.

1. UNDER THE LINE finger tracking helps students whose eyes are drawn downward. With this method, the finger points below the line of print. The reason Ann might benefit from encouragement to use her finger UNDER is because her eyes may tend to accidentally move down to the next line. So, when her hand covers the distractions that are below the line of print, her eyes won't be able to move down as easily and she may be able to stay visually focused on the correct line of print.

2. **ABOVE THE LINE tracking helps students whose eyes are drawn upward.** With this method, the finger points above the line of print. The reason Ann might benefit from encouragement to use her finger ABOVE is because her eyes may tend to accidentally move up to the next line. So, when her hand covers the distractions that are above the line of print, her eyes won't be able to move up as easily. As a result, she may be able to stay visually focused on the correct line of print.

3. LEFT MARGIN tracking helps students who have difficulty moving from one line of print to the next. With this method, the left-hand finger points to the beginning of each line of print along the left-hand margin. When Ann reaches the end of a row of print at the right side of the page, she "clicks" her left-hand finger down to the next row of print. This helps Ann to shift her eye gaze back to the left side of the page to where her finger has moved.

●▶ Strategy 2-6: Top-to-Bottom Scanning

"top-to-bottom scan"

"wavy scan"

Observed Behavior

Keisha can't find anything on the shelves, unless she is told the exact shelf on which to look. When she completes paper tasks, her attention jumps all over the page, so she misses items that she might have known.

Many students quickly start a task without giving any consideration to *how* they should approach it. If we randomly let our eyes jump all over an area, we will most likely miss seeing some things. To see and find everything in a given area, we must be systematic and have a plan for how we look at that area. The easiest way to be sure we have seen all there is to see is by *scanning* across sections one at a time. We also need to consistently scan in the same direction. As the world of print tends to go from left to right, it makes sense to learn to scan from left to right across a surface. To ensure that we cover the entire surface, we need to scan the top of an area, then the middle, and finally the bottom. This is called *top-to-bottom* scanning.

Strategies and Tools to Improve the Student's Performance

We need to teach students the strategy of scanning for the careful examination of scenes, objects, and so on, by practicing first on paper tasks. "Hidden picture" tasks are ideal sources for visual scanning practice. Students benefit initially from using their finger to point to where they are looking as they scan across parts of a picture. They should be encouraged to always scan in a left-to-right direction. To efficiently cover the entire area or section of the task at hand, their eyes will need to move in a "wavy" motion across a defined area. Students respond to the verbal reminder "wavy scan" by remembering to move their eyes and fingers across an area. So, a paper task divided into three major areas (top, middle, bottom) will require the completion of three "wavy scans."

However, the students may still "peek" down the page to mark something unless they are prevented from doing so. The easiest way to accomplish this is by creating an easy-to-handle cover that can be moved to expose only one section of the task at a time. The hidden-picture task will need to be marked (preferably with color markings) into sections and then placed under the cover with the top edge sticking out. The students can then pull up the paper to the marked line to view one section at a time. Each section can then be scanned with the "wavy" motion as hidden items are marked.

1. Perform sample paper tasks that can improve TOP-TO-BOTTOM scanning. Provide students with practice in training their eyes to scan paper tasks systematically, so they don't miss things. It's more motivating to use a "fun job," so an activity like hidden pictures can work well. Worksheets are provided at the end of this strategy to help students practice this skill. Choose one that is appropriate for the student's age and make thick red lines across the page to mark the sections. Use the following sample task to model top-to-bottom scanning.

Color 10 flowers.

2. Follow the directions below for making a student "pocket" (acetate sleeve) for hidden picture tasks. We want students to look at only one section at a time. To prevent them from peeking down the page, make a cover, or sleeve, for the task. That way, we can instruct the students to place the task in the sleeve and pull up one section of the paper at a time. To make the sleeve, we'll need a supply of plastic "report cover" sleeves and a non-see-through paper to cover the task. We can write or draw the instructions for using the "pocket" on the non-see-through cover sheet. Then instruct the students to place the hidden-picture task in the lined acetate sleeve with the top edge sticking up. An illustrated instruction guide for creating the sleeve is provided here.

Note: For the instructor's convenience, an enlargement of the students' page that will fit a standard-sized report cover is provided in the worksheets at the back of this strategy.

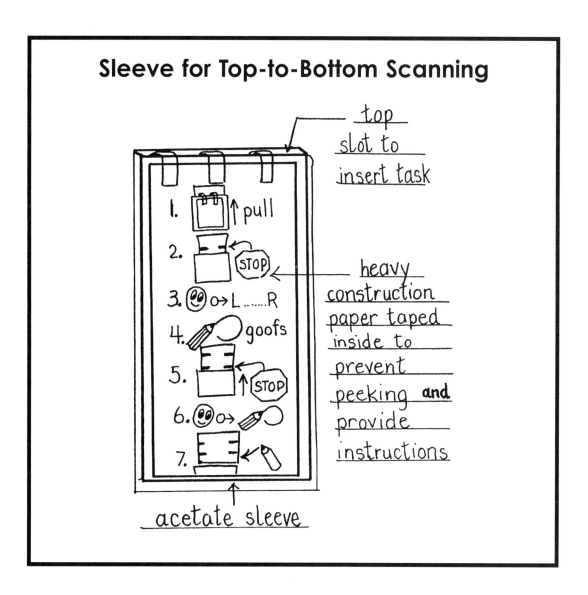

3. Create CUE CARDS to remind students to scan from top to bottom.
Place CUE CARDS in a visible place on the students' desks or on a bulletin board to remind them to start at the top, then move to the middle, and finally to the bottom section. Please note the arrows next to the picture, which the students can color.

Say: "Color the top arrow blue for the sky which is at the top of everything." This will remind the students to always scan the top section first.

Say: "Color the middle arrow green for the plants which are in the middle of the picture." This will remind the students that the middle part should be scanned next.

Say: "Now, color the bottom arrow brown for the ground or dirt which is at the bottom." This will remind the students to always scan the bottom section last.

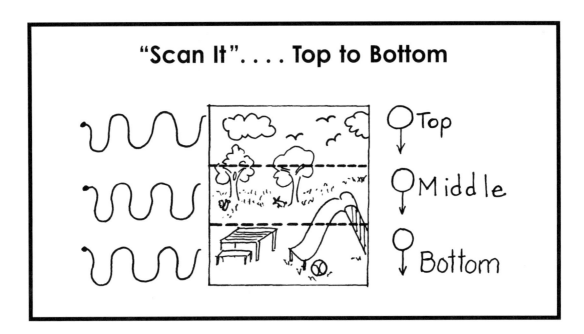

Worksheets

Top-to-Bottom Scanning for Beginning Level

- Color 10 things with circle shapes.
- Color 10 things with square shapes.
- Color 10 things with triangle shapes.
- Color 10 flowers.
- Color 10 things you can find at school.
- Color 10 things you can eat.

Color 10 things with circle shapes.

Name_____ Date_____

Color 10 things with square shapes.

Color 10 things with triangle shapes.

Name_____ Date_____

Color 10 flowers.

Color 10 things you can find at school.

Name_____ Date_____

Color 10 things you can eat.

Worksheets

Top-to-Bottom Scanning for Intermediate Level

- Color 10 Things Wrong with This Picture—1
- Color 10 Things Wrong with This Picture—2
- Color 10 Things Wrong with This Picture—3
- Color 10 Things Wrong with This Picture—4
- Color 10 Things Wrong with This Picture—5

Name_____ Date_____

Color 10 Things Wrong with This Picture—1

Sara loves her farm animals so much that she does not notice the 10 things that are wrong in the pasture. Can you find them?

Source: What's Wrong With This Picture by Anna Pomaska
(Dover Publications, Inc., New York, 1983). Used with permission.

Name_____ Date_____

Color 10 Things Wrong with This Picture—2

While Bobby and Leslie enjoy a teatime snack, they do not notice that 10 things are wrong around them. Can you see them?

Source: What's Wrong With This Picture by Anna Pomaska
(Dover Publications, Inc., New York, 1983). Used with permission.

Color 10 Things Wrong with This Picture—3

Peter is diving beneath the water while Sally is learning to swim above. They are both so absorbed in what they are doing that they do not see the 10 things around them that are wrong. Can you?

Source: What's Wrong With This Picture by Anna Pomaska
(Dover Publications, Inc., New York, 1983). Used with permission.

Color 10 Things Wrong with This Picture—4

As Mrs. Smith is cooking supper, 10 things are wrong in the kitchen. Can you discover them?

Source: What's Wrong With This Picture by Anna Pomaska
(Dover Publications, Inc., New York, 1983). Used with permission.

Color 10 Things Wrong with This Picture—5

Jane is too contented reading in bed to notice the 10 strange things in her bedroom. But maybe you can find them for her.

Source: What's Wrong With This Picture by Anna Pomaska
(Dover Publications, Inc., New York, 1983). Used with permission.

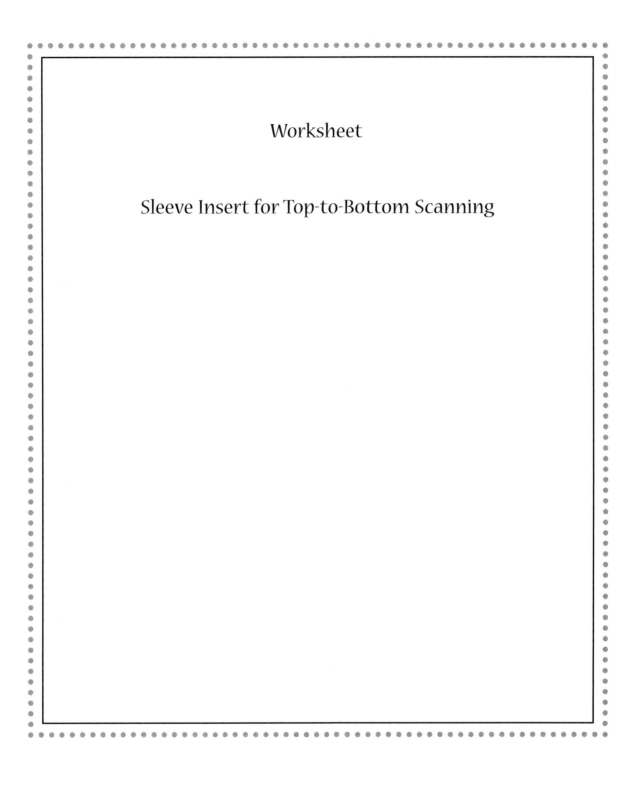

Worksheet

Sleeve Insert for Top-to-Bottom Scanning

1. pull up

2. stop on marks

3. **L**eft to **R**ight

4. circle goofs

5. pull up
   stop on marks

6.

7.

● Strategy 2-7: Margin Scanning "margin scan"

Observed Behavior

Rick seems to freeze when presented with a paper that contains multiple tasks. He won't start without someone's assistance. Even after he starts, he needs encouragement to continue to the next section of the paper.

Many students are quickly triggered into states of anxiety when the teacher passes out a paper with multiple tasks. All these students see is a jumble of words. Yet, some students instinctively scan a paper before beginning to work. This provides them with a sense of how difficult the tasks really are on the paper. It also lets them know how many parts, or separate sections, are on the single page. They are often relieved to find their initial reaction of "Wow, that looks hard!" was inaccurate. Instead, they discover that the task just *looked big*. Once students are able to scan a large task and break it into smaller parts, they will be better prepared to concentrate and to attend to one part at a time. If they are still overwhelmed by a particular task, they can be taught to skip over it, cover all the other tasks, and then return to the one (or ones) they found most difficult. The skill of systematically analyzing a paper before beginning can be easily taught.

Strategies and Tools to Improve the Student's Performance

We need to give Rick some sample worksheets and explain that we are going to teach him a new way to understand how to examine the page so he can see the different parts. Using examples, point out to him that most paper tasks have dark printed instructions that are often enlarged in size. Often, the instructions even begin in the left-hand margin of the paper, which makes them easier to detect. Between tasks, extra spaces are also often inserted to visually separate one task from the next. So, by using a finger to track down the left-side margin, a student can usually spot separate tasks. Once the number of tasks has been identified, and assuming that the tasks can be performed in any order, Rick will be able to select the task he wants to do first and cover the remaining tasks so he is not overwhelmed. As each task is completed, he can uncover the next task.

1. Follow recipe for margin scanning. Say: "Using your fingers and your eyes, scan down the left-hand margin." Continue saying:

- Pause when you notice a change in the print.
- Pause when you notice extra spaces between lines of print.

- Count how many jobs or tasks are on the whole page.
- Select the job you want to do first.
- Cover the other jobs until you are finished with the first.
- Continue doing the jobs until the page is done.

2. Practice page-layout scanning. Select a variety of typical classroom worksheets to practice the scanning of page layouts. Specific pages could be found to demonstrate: dark printed instructions, enlarged print for headings/directions, spaces between sections, and instructions that stick out into the left-hand margin.

3. Use a CUE CARD to remind students to use margin scanning. Place CUE CARDS such as the one that follows on the students' desks or post one on a bulletin board as a reminder to use the margin scanning strategy.

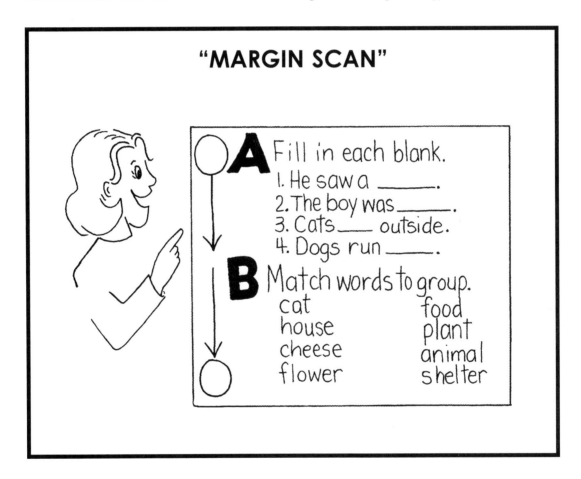

◆▶ Strategy 2-8: Page Layout Scanning "layout scan"

Observed Behavior

Jaime gets exhausted when completing a worksheet. By the time he is finished with the first section, he has no energy left for the second section. Sadly, the second section frequently turns out to be much easier than the initial part over which he struggled.

As we have seen, when students are faced with worksheet tasks, they can feel overwhelmed. Even knowing how many tasks there are on the page does not reduce their apprehension. They know they have trouble understanding printed instructions, so they remain baffled.

Strategies and Tools to Improve the Student's Performance

Students' anxieties can be reduced by teaching them how to recognize specific layouts, or formats. Many layouts, such as matching, are self-explanatory because they appear as two columns of words. Other layouts, such as fill-in-the-blanks, multiple choice, or word banks, can also become easily recognizable so as to make students feel more competent. Knowing what each type of task looks like will enable the students to choose which ones they want to do first. More difficult tasks that might require assistance can then be saved until later.

1. Follow the general instructions below for teaching layout-scanning skills. These should be followed in the order given.

- Choose some sample worksheet pages to illustrate different kinds of tasks.
- Draw the top-to-bottom arrow down the left-hand margin of each page.
- Ask the students to determine the number of tasks.
- Describe an example of a specific type of layout. This can be:
  - ▶ a matching task with columns,
  - ▶ a word-bank task with a box containing answer choices, or
  - ▶ multiple-choice tasks with one to three items from which to select a response.
- Ask the student to find and circle a specific type of task on the paper.
- Continue this procedure through all types of layouts.
- As a surprise, tell them they don't have to complete the tasks; you only wanted them to find them!

2. Perform the following group activity for layout scanning. Cut up worksheet pages into types of tasks and have the students sort them into boxes by the type of layout.

3. Create sample tasks for layout scanning. Cut out and glue together different types of layout tasks on a page. Ask students to find or mark specific types of layouts for printed tasks. Some examples might be: **Say:**

- "With your red marker, circle the 'word bank' task."

- "With your pencil, make a dotted line around the 'word bank' task."

- "With your pencil, make a circle (square, triangle, oval, etc.) around the 'word bank' task."

"Layout Scan"

A. Underline the right answer to each question.
 1. When did this story take place?
   a. during the summer
   b. in the daytime
   c. in the night time
   d. during the winter
 2. How many people were in the story?
   a. fifteen people
   b. ten people
   c. five people
   d. twelve people

B. Finish each sentence with a word from the word box.

excited	unhappy	galloped
carrots	stables	trotted
lessons	saddles	nature center

 1. The riding team met at the _____.
 2. The boys rubbed down the horses and fed them _____, when they were finished.
 3. The horses moved at a fast rate, as they _____ around the track.
 4. The boys were required to remove the horses' _____, when they were finished with the lesson.

C. When did these things happen? Write the words first, second or third.
 1. This happened _____. The boys removed the saddles from the horses.
 2. This happened _____. The boys got to the stables.
 3. This happened _____. The boys gave carrots to the horses after they were rubbed down.

D. Match the words that mean almost the same thing.
   gently   finished
   pleased   displeased
   event   expected
   take off   softly
   done   delighted
   unhappy   happening
   required   remove

◆ Strategy 2-9: Skip It . . . Come Back Later   "skip it"

Observed Behavior

Winona just sits there looking worried or anxious. She looks back at a confusing item, rereads it, and continues to worry. When time is up for the task, she says, "I'm not finished." All her time was wasted because she was stuck on the one troubling item and she felt she could not go on with other items until she completed the "worry" item.

Strategies and Tools to Improve the Student's Performance

Students often get anxious or "stuck" waiting for help. By circling an item, they can go on and be self-reminded by the visible mark of the circled item to recheck their work. Besides, on many types of worksheets, students will often find that there is only one word left when they get to the end of the task—and it fits the one that was skipped!

   1. Create a sample illustration or CUE CARD. Place the following CUE CARD on the students' desks or post it on a bulletin board as a reminder to use the "Skip it . . . come back later" strategy.

   2. Use bonus points to provide special motivation. When you see a student has circled an item and returned later to complete it, give him or her bonus points for using the strategy. Mark the student's paper at the top with a +1 "skip it" to encourage the strategy's continued use.

Strategy 2-10: Covering Items to Reduce Distraction   "cover it"

Observed Behavior

Alicia is doing a math facts paper. She sees some in the next row she knows, so she skips down the page to them. She forgets to go back later and fill in the row she skipped, thus missing an entire row on the paper.

Students can be easily distracted by nearby print. This is especially true with math papers. When they spot a problem down the page that they know, they jump down to that row. Then, instead of going back to the row they were on, they continue on the row to which they jumped. Often, they forget to come back and finish the row at the top of the page. If Alicia had covered those other rows, she would *not* have been tempted to jump ahead. By covering everything on the page except the one part they are working on, students can put all their concentration on that one section.

Strategies and Tools to Improve the Student's Performance

1. Create a math sample illustration or CUE CARD. This encourages the student to cover all but one row at a time, so there is less temptation to jump down to a problem that is easily recognized. The following illustration can be placed on a student's desk to remind him or her to use the "Cover It" strategy with math tasks.

2. Create a reading sample illustration or CUE CARD. This encourages students to cover nearby items that may be distracting to them. In this way, they can put their full concentration on one task part at a time. This illustration can also be placed on a student's desk as a reminder to use the "Cover It" strategy with reading tasks.

◆❯ Strategy 2-11: Tracing to Improve Accuracy   "trace it"

Observed Behavior

Ben gets a math worksheet to do but he doesn't read the directions. Instead, he completes all the problems using the process sign of the first problem. Thereafter he never looks at the process signs. With a mixed process sheet, he usually misses half of the problems.

Ben can be impulsive; he doesn't always look carefully at paper tasks. When performing math operations, he makes assumptions from the first item about what to do, instead of reading instructions. He also encounters the same difficulty with spelling because he doesn't check his written spelling. He does not notice the mis-ordering of letters within words, so he makes undiscovered—and unnecessary—errors. These types of errors indicate that Ben would benefit from encouragement to check his work through finger tracing rather than through re-looking.

When students are in a hurry or are impulsive, they often do not see what is actually there. They assume they have seen it correctly and are upset when they are told they got it wrong. Sadly, if they had seen it correctly the first time, they most likely would have gotten it right.

Strategies and Tools to Improve the Student's Performance

Tracing to Improve Math Accuracy

In math, when mixed operations ($+$, $-$, $\times$, $\div$) appear on the same task, students forget to carefully note the process signs. What if Ben were shown how to finger-trace or pencil-trace the process signs on math problems? By tracing with finger movement, which is a motor memory source, Ben might learn to recognize his errors.

Create a math sample illustration or CUE CARD. This sample illustration for math is meant to encourage students to trace over the signs, so they pay better attention to which processes are asked for on mixed problem sheets. It can be placed on the desks of those students who would benefit from a visual reminder of the "Trace It" strategy.

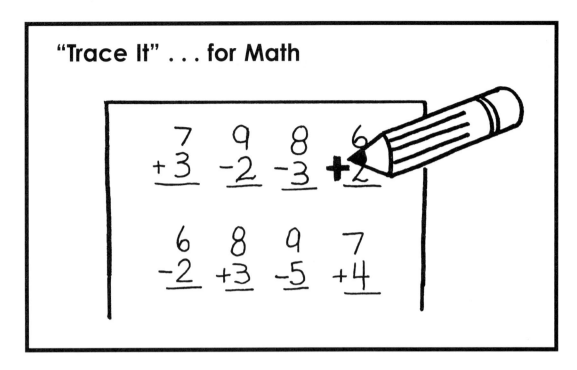

Note: A "surprise" way to teach this skill is to hand the students a large work-sheet of mixed problems without first telling them what they are going to do. Once they are ready to start, announce that they are not going to have to work the problems. They are *only* going to trace the signs with their pencils. This will show them how each mark (+, −, ×, ÷) has a different feel. Explain to them that this kind of tracing can help them to be more careful on mixed math papers. The act of tracing activates motor/skin awareness that may compensate for a student's weak visual attention for details.

Tracing to Improve Spelling Accuracy

In spelling, when the word on the paper "kind of" looks right, students often don't know how to check the actual letters they have written. What if the students were encouraged to trace the questionable spelling word or rewrite it with their fingers? Might they notice the word "feels" wrong and thus possibly recall the correct spelling? By tracing, they are appealing to motor memory for recall. This technique often helps students who can recognize when a word looks wrong, but who can't remember how the word should look in order to correct it. Instead of looking (visual), they switch to feeling (motor) to remember.

Create a sample illustration or CUE CARD. This sample illustration for spelling is meant to encourage students to trace over the word, so they pay better attention to words that "feel" wrong and possibly recall the correct spelling. It can be placed on the desks of students who would benefit from a visual reminder to use this "Trace It" strategy.

◆▶ Strategy 2-12: Talk It . . . Audibly "talk it"

Observed Behavior

When Susan reads, she has difficulty figuring out new words, so she tends to substitute a familiar word that begins with the same first letter as the printed word that is troubling her. Because Susan does not recognize that the word she selected makes no sense in the sentence, she does not know to correct it.

Strategies and Tools to Improve the Student's Performance

Students are often unaware of their errors in reading. As a result, their reading comprehension suffers greatly. If Susan had been able to recognize her errors, she might have corrected them. Students should be encouraged to experiment with a "talk it" system. When we talk just loud enough for our own ears to hear, we can read more accurately. Our ears recognize when the reading "sounds funny." Sometimes, we may even grimace in response to the nonsense we hear coming into our ear. It's a signal to stop. ("Oops . . . better check it.") We learn to go back to re-read it to find the error. When we've heard the sentences correctly from re-reading, the flow of reading improves. We can even begin to make a movie of the story reading in our head. The end result often is a boost in reading comprehension and an increase in self-confidence.

The following illustrations of these strategies can be copied as charts or CUE CARDS as reminders for the students to use the strategies.

1. Create a "talk it" illustration. This illustration should be placed on the students' work areas, so they will be reminded to use their "whispered" voice as they perform a task. In this way, students can hear the "echo" of their own words in their ears and monitor the accuracy of what they are doing and reading.

2. Create a "fix it" illustration. This illustration reminds the students to fix the "goofs" they hear in the task they are "whispering." This is especially helpful in reading and written language tasks. It is also an essential part of editing of rough drafts on writing assignments. By listening to what they actually have written, students can identify what is missing.

Strategy 2-13: Marking Items   "mark it"

Observed Behavior

Ali can read at a higher than expected grade level because he is good at figuring out most unknown words using sentence-meaning clues. Even when he has to skip words, he understands most of the story. His main idea comprehension is very good, but he always has difficulty with the follow-up questions about the descriptive details and the vocabulary.

Strategies and Tools to Improve the Student's Performance

During their reading, students often encounter unknown vocabulary words. But to stop and ask what a word means while in the midst of reading would interfere with the flow of ideas or cause the need to re-read. Although teachers do not like to encourage writing in textbooks, some suggest that students make small pencil marks in the margins to note unknown vocabulary words in the process of reading. If the pencil marks are made with a soft pencil, they are often not even visible after erasure. Students could also use the newly designed highlighters that have "rub-off" transparent tape. New "mini-sticky notes" can also be used, asking students to place one near the unknown word so that they can easily find the word or words when they return to them. Using these techniques, the student could continue reading without breaking the flow and return later to ask an adult to explain the meaning of the word. In some instances, by reading on, students may even figure out the meaning of the unknown word without help from others or without the use of a reference tool. Should this be an observably successful strategy for a specific student, a simple reminder to always have a pencil, highlighter, or sticky notes in hand while reading would ensure that the student remembers to make marks on the line where an unknown vocabulary word appears as he or she reads. Later, vocabulary cards could be created for the student's individual word bank.

While in the midst of reading, students might be interrupted by someone else asking them a question. Looking up from the text will likely make it necessary for the students to re-read or find their place. Reading is hard enough for some students without the added burden of making them re-read. Instead, why not make a small mark in the margin, attach a sticky note near the word, or place a pointing finger on the line of print at which the interruption occurred? With this strategy, students can return directly to the point at which they stopped reading.

Create a CUE CARD to remind students to use vocabulary marking and place marking.

"MARK IT"

To save your place or mark
new vocabulary words as you read

●❯ Strategy 2-14: Snake Your Paper   "snake it"

Observed Behavior

Song finishes her work rapidly because she wants to be the first one done. But in her rush to get finished, she often accidentally skips items or rows of items. She is always confused when her papers are returned with items marked incorrect.

Most students are so tired, depleted, or bored after finishing a task that they have no energy left for checking it before they turn it in to the teacher—or so it appears. More often, the truth is they do not have a learned system for rapidly checking a completed task to make sure they have not accidentally skipped any items. The majority of students would be highly motivated to self-check their work if they saw an immediate chance to increase their grades.

Strategies and Tools to Improve the Student's Performance

"Snaking the paper" is a visual-motor strategy for checking all areas of a worksheet for empty spaces. Initially, this strategy is best demonstrated with an overhead in the classroom or individually with a student. Empty spaces usually mean an item has been overlooked. "Snaking" is done with the pointer finger that slides slowly back and forth across each row of print. The resulting movement feels like a slithering snake going down the page. The finger is not lifted. Instead, the finger moves to the end of one line and then goes backward on the next line down the page and continues back and forth until the end of the page. Should an empty space be identified, the student is alerted to check if it is an answer space and, if so, to complete the item.

1. Follow the general instructions below for "snake checking" a completed task. First, tell the students they do *not* have to read their paper. Then, **say** and visually demonstrate:

"Slide the finger back and forth down the page."
"Pause for spaces."
"Stop when an empty space is noticed."
"Fill in the answer."
"Continue snaking until the entire page is done."

2. Practice on papers to master "snake checking." Initially, this skill can be practiced on papers that have not been completed. With a marker, have the student carefully snake each row of print, going back and forth down the page, and color the answer lines. On completion, **say:** "There should have been twenty-three answer spaces. Did you find them all?"

3. Use the following motivational device to encourage practice with "snake checking." On selected tasks, offer the students the chance to earn bonus points.

> **Say:** "Does anyone want to earn a Checking Bonus Point? If you do, raise your hand, so I can mark your paper with a 'B for Bonus' at the top." Some won't want to and that's okay. Just have them turn over their paper.

> **Say:** "When I say 'ready, go,' we'll all SNAKE the page."

4. Create a CUE CARD to remind students to use "snake checking" for reading. The following CUE CARD can be copied for charts or specific students' desktops as a signal to remember to use the strategy for locating missing spaces or "gaps" on the paper.

5. Create a CUE CARD to remind students to use "snake checking" for math. The following CUE CARD can be copied for charts or specific students' desk-tops as a signal to remember to use the strategy. This suggestion is included because many students tend to spot problems they can answer down near the bottom of papers and forget to go back to finish the row or rows they skipped. This illustration should be copied for those students who need this reminder.

Section Three

Memory-Enhancing Strategies

· · · · · · · · · · · · · · · · · · · ·

What's Involved in Being Able to Remember?

Every student develops a specific and personalized way of remembering, so, as instructors, we must be observant if we are to recognize a student's unique memory strengths. Is he or she most successful as a speaker? a socializer? a listener, a speller, a reader, or a writer? Such students are often adept in a world of words—reading, listening, reading, writing, and speaking. They are also likely to be skilled at the kind of thinking that requires analysis and sequencing of parts that make up a whole. This type of student is most likely a *verbal learner*.

Or, is the student most successful as a builder, a doodler, an artist, a computer whiz, a puzzle solver, or a mathematician? Such students are often adept in the world of vision, graphics, and spatial organization. They are also likely to be skilled at the kind of thinking that requires synthesis and noting the whole concept. This type of student is often called a *visual learner*.

Or, perhaps the student is most successful as a sensor, a mover, or a feeler. These students are often adept in the world of movement and touch. They are likely to be skilled at the kind of thinking that requires exploration through experience or actually feeling and manipulating objects. This type of student is often labeled a *tactile-kinesthetic learner*.

Each of these modes for gaining information has the potential to become a strength that can be utilized by students to increase their comprehension and memory.

No one is 100 percent a "hear-er," "see-er," or "feel-er." Yet for each person, one style, or mode, of remembering is typically stronger than the others. Sometimes, however, students can have a memory strength that combines two modes. Once they have identified their preferred mode for remembering—be it a single or a paired mode—students can use it to comprehend or understand essential information in a manner that will make it easier to recall at a later time. When faced with a frustrating task, they can change the task to include their preferred memory strength, making the task easier to perform. For example, a weak visual learner who is attempting to perform a complex math task could talk the process through orally and switch to using a "hearing" mode rather than being forced to "see" how to do it. The student would, of course, have to remember to switch to talking about the math problem rather than just viewing or looking at it.

Many students almost instinctively use their most developed memory strength without being aware that they are doing so. Struggling students, however, often cannot identify their memory strengths. Or, they cannot recognize when it would be helpful to apply a particular strategy that utilizes their memory strengths to improve their learning. Our job as instructors is to observe the students having successful learning experiences so we can identify the strategies they employed to capitalize on their probable memory strengths. With the strengths identified, we can more efficiently select and demonstrate other strategies that will further increase their memory. As memory increases, so, too, does success—and with success comes increased confidence.

Once the students have learned to successfully take in information and understand it through their preferred memory mode, they will likely be able to recall the information for a short time immediately following the instruction. This kind of memory is called *short-term memory* because typically it can be remembered for only a short time. It is not permanently encoded in their memory "storehouse." Short-term memory is essential in that it provides a short amount of time for the brain to begin to interpret and comprehend the new information. But the difficulty with short-term memory is that the newly acquired information can literally fall out of one's head if it isn't clarified, re-examined, or used. The failure of short-term memory is not unlike the feeling older students get when they have put in an "all-nighter" cramming for a test. After hours of memorizing, their greatest fear is that someone will ask a question that rattles them, thus causing last night's learning to crumble apart and fall out of memory. Our job as instructors is to make certain that students are not cramming half-understood information into their minds. Moreover, it is essential that we help students discover their preferred memory style so they can gain as much information as possible from our instruction on a "short-term" basis.

Once students are able to learn new information through their short-term memory, we must help them discover ways to transfer the new information into *long-term memory*. Transferring information solidly into long-term memory is the only way to guarantee that a person will be able to find, or recall, information over time. Typically, people put information randomly into their heads—much like last-minute memorization—without taking the time to hook ideas together. The ideas float around without a place to land. Such ideas are hard to retrieve later. This is comparable to creating a document on a computer and forgetting to save it to a file with related documents; later it will be impossible to find. To truly master "new" information, it is necessary to associate it with "old" learning and thus hook it solidly into a category, or file, of knowledge in our brain's "computer bank" filing system. Students will benefit from instruction about strategies that will improve their ability to hook new and old knowledge together. These strategies are generally called association techniques. Over time, students continue to hook new learning together with old learning to create clusters, or categories, of memories. As a result—like a computer—their memory storehouse develops an intricate organizational system that enables them to search and find information without experiencing excessive frustration.

How Are the Memory Strategies Organized?

The strategies in this section include techniques that are more complex than those in Section 2 on enhancing attention. There is more of an in-depth discussion on and description of how and why each strategy works, based on the functions and processes of the brain. By gaining a greater understanding of the more technical information on how memory does and does not function in the brain, instructors can better understand how to teach students these new techniques. Initially, the strategies may appear to be difficult to teach; as a result, "recipes" with step-by-step instructions and samples are included. Each strategy can be taught to small groups of students who have been specifically identified as those most likely to benefit from the strategy based on the students' preferred memory strengths.

To increase the instructor's ability to efficiently select strategies from this section, the strategies are clustered into four categories: verbal-learner strategies, visual-learner strategies, paired-memory-learner strategies, and multimodality-learner strategies. As a result, instructors need to realize, for example, that a strategy found in the visual category might not be the most effective for a verbal-memory learner. Likewise, a student who has moderate learning difficulties would be more likely to benefit from the use of a multimodality strategy rather than a single-memory mode strategy. When many modes of memory are simultaneously stimulated, information is spread throughout the memory centers of the brain. Therefore, there may be more areas into which the information can be stored and more easily recalled at a later time.

Even when a memory strategy appears to be near mastery, students often need to be reminded to initiate its use. Suggestions for quick verbal reminder statements are listed in quotation marks directly after each strategy heading. In addition, you will find sample CUE CARDS which provide picture illustrations for each strategy. Copying and placing the CUE CARDS in the students' environment gives them a visual reminder to use the new strategy without the embarrassment of an adult "bugging" them. When you observe students using their strategy, do not forget to acknowledge and commend their independent attempts to do so. Praise will naturally lead the students to more active use of the strategy and thus the strategies become practiced and mastered without further need of reminders.

◆❯ Strategy 3-1: Rehearse Important Words in Instruction   "rehearse it" or "echo"

Observed Behavior

Willie is trying his best to concentrate on the instructions his teacher is giving about the next task the class will do. Every time the teacher starts giving an instruction, Willie gets anxious. He heard her say he needed his reading book. While searching in his desk for the book, he doesn't remember the page number she said. Did she say what part of the page he was to do? He does not know for sure. Instead of asking for help, he has learned it is less embarrassing to watch Susie, who sits next to him.

Willie is having great difficulty remembering what his teacher has just asked him to do. His difficulty is based on the speed at which his brain can register, or encode, the rapidly incoming sound information. For many children, the old saying "In one ear and out the other" is all too true. The sound is just too fast for Willie to hold on to long enough to fully comprehend. So instead of getting all the directions, he usually remembers only the first part, "Get out your reading book." Willie needs more opportunities to hear the instruction so he can truly remember it, but his teacher cannot always be there to repeat instructions for him.

Strategies and Tools to Improve the Student's Performance

Willie might benefit from learning a special way to "repeat" instructions to himself. Having the chance to repeat the most important words in instructions, or "rehearsing" them, his brain would have a chance to hear it again. When we are using *rehearsal*, the sound of our words go back around and re-enter our ears to reactivate the hearing system in our brain one more time, building a stronger memory of the information. Yet we don't want Willie to repeat everything he hears. We want him to re-hear only the most essential words that he needs to complete the instruction successfully.

1. Teach the two basic skills needed to learn the rehearsal strategy.
First, students must be able to identify exactly which of the words they hear are absolutely essential if they are to perform the task successfully. Learning to select

the relevant words from within longer sentences takes practice. In a large group, or with a trusted teacher, students are less embarrassed by possible mistakes and more willing to actively participate in rehearsal tasks.

Second, students must be able to repeat, or rehearse, the selected words in a "whispered" voice. When they are first learning to rehearse, students may need to repeat the important words a number of times while they are performing the task.

2. Follow these directions to teach "Rehearsal."

First, obtain a worksheet from a standard "following directions" workbook. These tasks are normally set up with an illustration at the top and specific directions to be completed at the bottom of the page.

Second, cut the illustration section off and copy it for the student. You keep the printed directions. Because the students won't be reading the task, you can select worksheets by interest level instead of worrying about your students' reading level.

3. Use the recipe below to instruct students about rehearsal.

- Give the students only the illustration section.

- Explain they are going to learn a strategy called "Rehearsal" (and describe it).

- Explain you will read one direction at a time about what to do to the picture.

- Tell students their job is to decide which words are most important to remember.

- Read each direction slowly.

- Ask students to identify and call out the most important words. By making it a group activity, children who are typically afraid to call out may be more willing to participate. Just listening to other children's responses can help students understand how to choose what is important.

- Name or list the important words they called out (usually no more than four).

- Tell students to repeat the words like an "echo" after you say them.

- Remind students to say the words in a "whispered" voice.

- Tell students to keep saying the words as they complete the directions.

- Repeat the procedure for each item.

4. Use the following sample task to model the "Rehearsal" strategy.

PATTY THE PLATYPUS

- Draw more fur on Patty. Some lines have been done for you.
- Color Patty's fur black.
- Color her beak and webbed feet a light brown.
- Draw one egg to the left of her. A platypus hatches from an egg, but is not a bird.
- Color three waves of water under Patty.
- Color the waves blue.
- Measure Patty from the tip of her beak to the end of her tail. She is ____ inches long. Write the number on the line at the bottom of the page.

--✁

She is ____ inches long.

"Patty the Platypus" is adapted from Katherine Hall, *Reading Stories for Comprehension Success*, Primary Level, published by The Center for Applied Research in Education (1996).

When at school, many students, in the moment of listening, may forget that they know how to repeat the most important instruction words to help them remember. They may need a reminder to "activate" this strategy. A visible reminder in the form of an illustration, perhaps placed on their desk, could be helpful.

5. Create an illustrated reminder (CUE CARD) for "repeat it" or "echo."

The CUE CARD could be copied and taped to the students' desks or attached to a bulletin board. The students could also be signaled with a short verbal clue like "Rehearse it," "Repeat it," or "Echo" (for younger students).

When at home, listening frustration also causes difficulty for students, as when their parents yell out to them, "Don't forget to bring your gym shorts, shoes, and the homework on your desk" as they all rush out in the morning. It's just too much information, at too rapid a rate, for many students to keep track of while they are doing something else. Mom or Dad could remind their children to repeat the instructions, using a quick statement such as "Say it again to remember" or "What did I say?" Ideally, the parent could repeat the important words in a list for the child to "echo." To encourage repeated use of the strategy, the child should be praised when he or she responds by repeating the words.

Worksheets

"Rehearsal" Practice

Three practice worksheets are included to illustrate how tasks can be chosen for the students' interest level. All the activities are on map studies, but each one is obviously at a different map-skill level.

Note: Remember to distribute *only* the illustration portion of the worksheet.

- The Teddy Bears' Campsite
- North America Map (two pages)
- A Weather Map

Name_____ Date_____

The Teddy Bears' Campsite

1. Put an X on the island.
2. Color the trees green.
3. Color the water blue.
4. Put a box around the mountains.
5. Draw a pine tree between the teddy bears and the lake.
6. Find the tent south of the picnic area. Color it brown.
7. Find the trees north of the picnic table. Draw a circle around them.
8. Draw a red line from the small tent to the group of pine trees in the West.
9. Draw a black line going to the East from the picnic table to the campfire.
10. Draw your favorite food on top of the picnic table.

North America Map

1. Label the four edges of your map: NORTH, SOUTH, EAST, and WEST.

2. Label the PACIFIC OCEAN, the ATLANTIC OCEAN, the ARCTIC OCEAN, and the GULF OF MEXICO.

3. Color the water on your map blue. (Don't forget about the GREAT LAKES and HUDSON BAY.)

4. Label CANADA and color it green.

5. Label MEXICO and color it brown.

6. Label CENTRAL AMERICA and color it orange.

7. Make a black dot (●) to show where LOS ANGELES, CALIFORNIA, is. Label it.

8. Make a dot for CHICAGO, ILLINOIS, and label it.

9. Mark and label NEW YORK, NEW YORK.

10. Make a red star to show where you live.

11. Color the UNITED STATES yellow. (Remember, ALASKA is part of the U.S.)

North America

A Weather Map

A weather map can tell you many things about the weather in many places. Most newspapers print a weather map each day. These maps are made by the United States Weather Bureau. If you know how to read a map, you can forecast the weather.

Symbols are used on maps. For example, numbers are used to tell the temperature at the time the map was made. This chart shows the symbols for sky conditions.

○ clear	® rain
◐ partly cloudy	Ⓢ snow
● cloudy	Ⓕ fog

An arrow attached to the sky condition tells the wind speed. Each long line on the arrow means 10 mph (miles per hour). Each short line means 5 mph. This symbol tells us that the sky is partly cloudy and the wind speed is 35 mph ◐⟍⟍⟍ .

✂ -

Draw a green line to connect the two cities that have partly cloudy weather.

You need to bring an umbrella when you visit this city: _____.

The sky condition in San Francisco today is _____. Draw a gray circle around the city.

Color the city with the highest temperature reading yellow.

Color the city with the lowest temperature reading blue.

The temperature in Seattle is _____.

Draw a brown line to connect the cities with 25-mph wind speeds.

Draw a black line to connect the cities with 10-mph wind speeds.

Name the city that has the lightest wind speed: _____.

◆ Strategy 3-2: Thinking Out Loud to Solve
Problems   "talk it" or "use your script"

Observed Behavior

Rolando is staring at his paper that has very complex subtraction problems containing large multidigit numbers that require borrowing or regrouping. Although he is trying to do the problems, he is getting lost in the steps of borrowing. He is getting frustrated to the point of tears, but does not ask for help.

Strategies and Tools to Improve
the Student's Performance

If Rolando has a memory strength for verbal information, he could be encouraged to use the strategy of "thinking out loud" to master the borrowing process in subtraction. In a moment of frustration, he could switch from looking at the confusing problems to "talking" through the process of borrowing step-by-step.

To do this, students can learn a very specific script for the steps. A *script* can be learned for any complex task that requires a specific order. A script's sole purpose is to provide a memory tool for performing a sequence in the correct order.

Note: The script presented here as a strategy for borrowing in subtraction also can be used as a guide for making any other type of script.

Before developing any script, the instructor must first be sure that the student has mastered the concepts related to the skill. A script will not help a student who does not understand the underlying concepts of the skill. The script for borrowing in subtraction demands that students understand the concept that the values of numbers change when they are in different positions within a larger multidigit number. Students can better understand this concept if they imagine each digit of a multidigit number placed in a house on a street, with each house (going from right to left) having money with increasing tens value. So, when we borrow, we go to our "next-door neighbor's" house, where there are bigger kinds of bills or currency. We ask if our neighbor has any money available from which we could borrow. Once the "next-door neighbor" has lent us money, we must cross out the number we started with and write in a number that is one less, because we only need to take one of the larger valued bills. Then we are on our way back to our own house with the extra money which will allow us to subtract. However, because the "next-door neighbor's" house has money with higher values than our own money, we must trade in the money we borrowed from our neighbor for the kind of money we have in our house before we add it to our house. In our decimal system, we will always trade in a larger bill for ten of the smaller bills.

The easiest way to help Rolando learn a script for this very complex sequence is to provide him with an easy-to-understand illustration of the houses in which he can place the numbers of a subtraction problem. Once he discovers that borrowing is like going to his next-door neighbor, he will have a concrete picture on which to build his script.

1. Use the illustrated grid below for borrowing from the "next-door neighbor." This will help Rolando solve the problem 362 – 195.

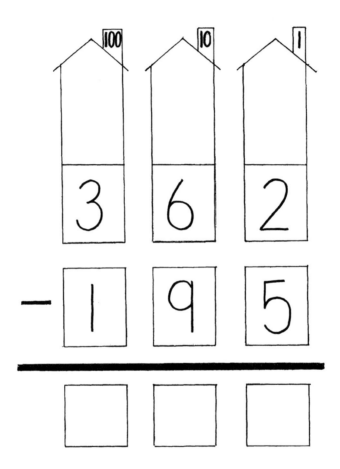

You will notice that the houses have two stories, so the students will have extra space for writing in the borrowed numbers. The second story should be eliminated when the skill is learned. For your convenience, a sample worksheet for the illustration (without numbers) is found at the end of this strategy section.

2. Use a script for borrowing in subtraction. Now that Rolando has seen his subtraction problem more clearly through the "houses" illustration, he is ready to learn a script. Initially, the instructor should model the use of the script while the student visually tracks the step-by-step process on the illustration of the "houses" with a pencil point. After following the script for one complete problem, the student should attempt to say the next problem in unison with the instructor. The student should be encouraged to say the script in a whispered voice to improve his self-monitoring of the steps.

This is Rolando's beginning script for the illustrated problem (362 – 195). With practice, Rolando will shorten it.

- "I can't take $5 from $2, so I must go next door to borrow from my neighbor. Does my neighbor have any money?"

- "He has 6 bills, but I need only 1, because they are ten-dollar bills."

- "That leaves 5 ten-dollar bills in my neighbor's house, but 10 one-dollar bills for me when I trade in the ten-dollar bill I borrowed."

- "With his 10 dollars and my 2 dollars, I now have 12 dollars. If I take away 5 dollars, that leaves 7 dollars."

- "Next column, I can't take 9 from 5, so I must go next door again. Does my neighbor have any money?"

- "He has 3 hundred-dollar bills, but I need only 1."

- "That leaves 2 hundred-dollar bills in his house, but 10 ten-dollar bills for me when I trade in the hundred-dollar bill I borrowed."

- "With his 10 ten-dollar bills and my 5 ten-dollar bills, I have 15 ten-dollar bills. If I take away 9, that leaves 6."

- "Next column is easy, I don't need to borrow: 2 take away 1 leaves 1."

Once the script is mastered for borrowing from digits 1–9, it should be modified for multidigit numbers that include zero digits in houses. Borrowing from a zero, or an empty house, means students will need to keep going up the street until they find a house with money. It is helpful to remind students about the rule for borrowing that states, "When you are going back to your house with the borrowed money, you must stop at each house along the way." Given this rule, students may remember that they will have to bring back the borrowed bill to the zero, or empty house, before they can proceed with the sequence. The empty house would then have ten from which a student could borrow. The script will need to be changed for "empty houses."

While students are initially learning this script, it is more effective for them to make *marks above numbers* showing the progression to and from number houses in columns. The marking on numbers is very important, because it gives students a visible path for re-checking, should they get interrupted midway through the process. The marking also reduces the length of a script because the student's pencil is doing some of the steps.

3. *Optional:* **Use a marking system for borrowing in subtraction.**

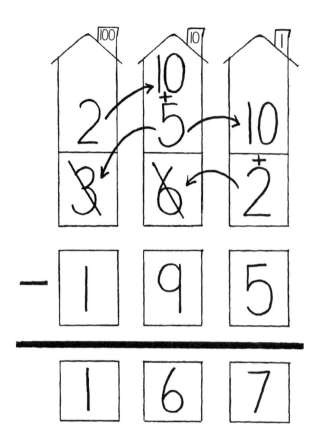

- This sample could be copied to send home for practice with parents.

- This sample could be enlarged to create a chart as a permanent model for students to consult when they are confused. It may be helpful to color-code the marks by columns. For example, the arrows going to and from the ones column to the tens column could be one color and the arrows going to and from the hundreds column could be a contrasting color.

4. Use a money kit to demonstrate borrowing. The borrowing process can be more interactive when students are encouraged to use a money kit as a "bank" for trading. The instructor will need a set of number cards that have a one-less digit written on the back and a desk-mat with three large column areas labeled as hundreds, tens, and one. The students can be asked to set up a three-digit number with the number cards in the correct columns and then place the correct amount of money under each digit. Then, they will be instructed to place the subtracting number cards in the next row. The script can then be practiced with students actively trading-in a larger bill for smaller bills. As bills are borrowed from under the cards, the student will turn over the card to see the one-less number.

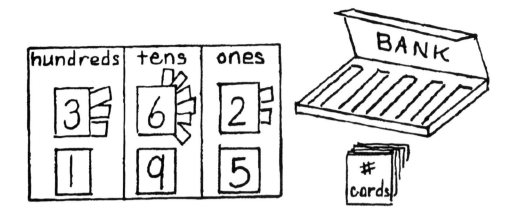

5. Create a CUE CARD to illustrate "talk it for borrowing" in subtraction. Even when students are successful in applying the "talk it" strategy to subtraction, they tend to forget to use it when frustrated. They will need a reminder. The following CUE CARD can be copied for placement on a desk or a bulletin board. (A visual reminder is less embarrassing to students.)

Worksheets

Using "Talk It" Strategy in Subtraction
with Next-Door Houses

Included first is a single problem page for the initial instruction of this concept. The next sample contains houses for four problems. The last sample contains six problems, but you will notice the last four problems on the page do not have roof lines, as most students will no longer need to have the support of the picture to understand the process at this point.

- Single substraction problem
- Four problems
- Six problems

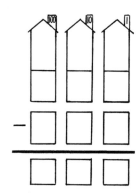

Name_____ Date_____

Borrow from Your Next-Door Neighbor

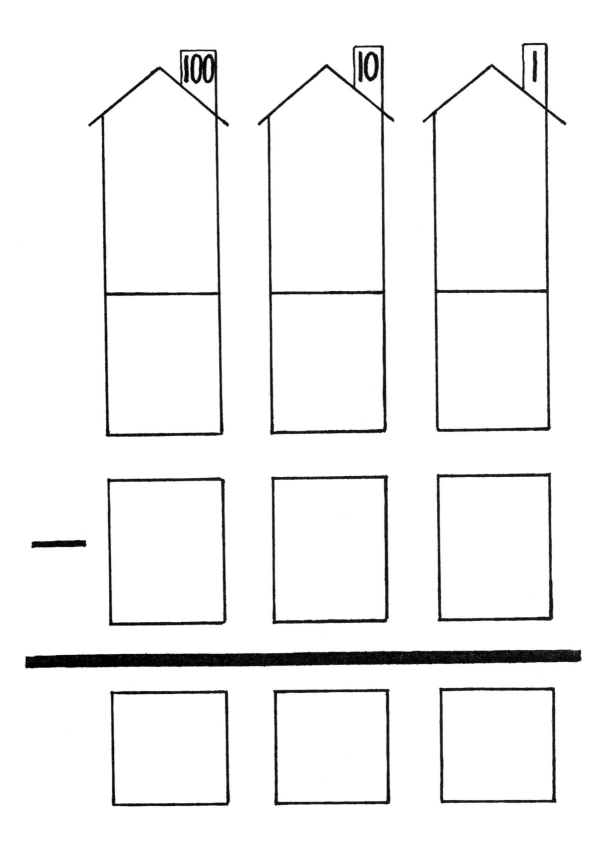

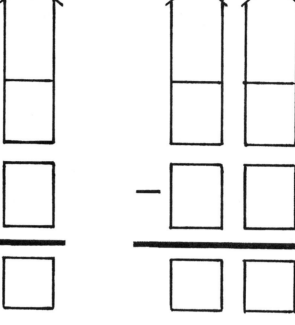

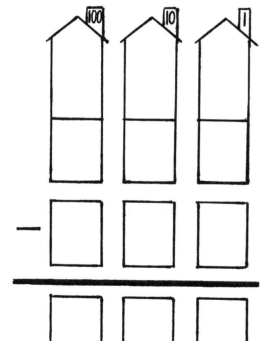

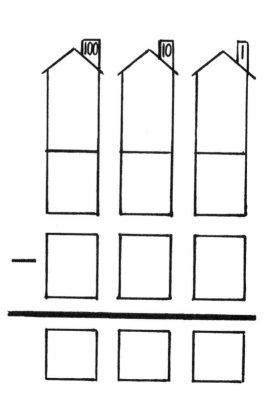

● Strategy 3-3: Highlighting Key Words in Reading
"highlight it"

Observed Behavior

Sheila has just finished reading the first unit in a new chapter of her science text. It has taken extra time because there were a lot of new vocabulary words to interpret and understand. Although Sheila can answer a majority of the teacher's questions on the main ideas in the section, she is not able to answer any of the questions about specific new details. She had to re-read whole sections to find the answers to unit questions. After persisting through three question searches, however, she gave up because she was just too tired to re-read any more text to search for the rest of the answers.

Sheila is not alone. Many students are only able to comprehend the general information and themes within a reading passage. Remember, there are two types of memory: short term and long term. On a first reading, Sheila is putting a large amount of general information into her short-term memory, as evidenced by her ability to recall a majority of the main ideas. Unfortunately, the new and more detailed information is not getting hooked into her existing knowledge base. However, good readers like Sheila can often recognize the detailed information when they are permitted to see it again. Sheila might benefit from being provided with a highlighting tool that permits rapid re-scanning, so she could efficiently review the content.

Strategies and Tools to Improve the Student's Performance

This style of selecting only essential information is called *target highlighting*. With the use of target highlighting, Sheila is encouraged to select words or phrases she believes are facts she will need to study for later testing. Because this system of highlighting puts extra emphasis on selecting only what is personally new, the student will need to decide if a specific word is really important enough to warrant highlighting. This skill can be learned as a small-group reading comprehension task. The small group could discuss the importance of a selected word, its newness, or its likelihood of actually appearing on a test. Because the skill of identifying relevant information takes time to learn, initially students will usually need to pause at the end of each sentence to determine if a word is so important that it must be highlighted.

After a few practice sessions, students usually notice their improved recall of reading facts. Given practice "mini-tests," they are amazed at how much information they can remember from just one reading when they have used target highlighting. The results of highlighting sessions with follow-up mini-tests help reinforce the students' motivation to persist in mastering the skill. With practice, the need for excessive highlighting decreases and small, irrelevant, and repeated words are skipped automatically. Over time, most students learn to pause only at the ends of paragraphs and then select five to ten words in each paragraph of standard high school text.

Additionally, whenever a student pauses to think "Is this word really important?" concentrated attention is dramatically increased on those words that are being considered. This in turn will enhance students' memory of the information. Finally, once students have mastered the skill of selecting only the words that are essential, students end up with a reduced number of highlighted words on a page. With target highlighting mastered, Sheila would then be able to more rapidly re-scan the reading content because she would not need to re-read the entire text. Instead, she would be able to re-read only the highlighted words and phrases to locate and review an important term.

1. **Use this recipe for target highlighting.**

   - Copy a section of "chapter-like" text (approximately 6–10 paragraphs).
   - Explain prior to doing the task:
     - Target highlighting focuses on identifying *only* new terms or details that will require additional study. Known terms will be skipped.
     - All the small, irrelevant, or repeated words won't be highlighted.
     - The end result of this strategy will be improved memory.
     - A bonus of using this strategy will be the ability to re-scan highlighting for review instead of re-reading everything.
   - Work with students on one sentence at a time for one paragraph.
     - Demonstrate how to select words that would be highlighted.
     - Demonstrate/explain why specific words would not be highlighted.
     - Discuss results when the target words have been chosen.
     - Assist with selecting and marking agreed-upon items.
     - Re-read the highlighted words in the paragraph to demonstrate oral scanning as a quick means of reviewing reading content.
   - Instruct students to work independently on the next two paragraphs.
     - Give permission to ask for help if needed.
     - When group finishes, discuss words selected. Why were they chosen?

▶ Ask if any of the words could have been skipped.

▶ Ask if any words that were forgotten should have been included.

- Work as independently as possible on next two paragraphs and discuss results.

- Ask the group to "whisper" their re-scanning of the highlighted words.

- Ask the group to turn over papers and do "mini-test" of oral question on the content.

  ▶ In mini-test, permit students to re-scan highlighting if they are stuck on questions.

- After the mini-test, ask students if:

  ▶ The highlighting helped build their memory.

  ▶ The highlighting helped them re-find information quicker.

- Repeat the procedure the next day on the unfinished text (4–5 paragraphs).

- Complete the section with a follow-up mini-test and re-scanning of highlighting.

- Remind students that highlighting is personal; they don't have to select the words their friend selects.

On page 139 is a sample of Sheila's completed target-highlighting task.

Note: In this sample, the highlighting choices are underlined because the process of copying does not allow for highlighting in color. However, using a color highlighting system is preferable because it is easier to re-scan visually.

There Lives a Monster in the Loch

The eerie dark depths of <u>Loch Ness</u>, <u>Scotland</u> invites the imagination to <u>conjure</u> visions of slithering, flesh-eating monsters. The mile-wide ribbon of water runs <u>23 miles</u> with a maximum depth of <u>754 feet</u>. Situated in the center of the <u>valley</u> of <u>Glenmore</u>, steep <u>wooded</u> mountains <u>rim</u> the lake. Rising <u>2,284 feet</u>, <u>Mealfourvonie Mountain</u> stands guard. The water itself is murky, stained with <u>peat</u>, and maintains a chilling temperature of <u>42 degrees F</u>.

For centuries, <u>legend</u> reports a monster living in the lake. These creatures are not unusual in <u>Scottish</u> and <u>Irish folklore</u>. Many <u>Celtic myths</u> dating as far back as the <u>tenth century</u> tell of <u>kelpies</u> living in waters throughout the region. The heads resemble that of a horse, hence the common name "<u>horse-eels</u>." Some observers compare the two raised ears to that of the horns, or <u>tentacula</u>, of a snail.

Popular theories compare the monster to <u>plesiosaurs</u> (marine reptiles of the dinosaur age). A sighting in <u>1933</u> by Mr. and Mrs. <u>Spicer</u> describes such a creature lumbering onto the shore of the lake. Horrified, the couple watched the monster snatch a lamb in its sharp-toothed mouth, then return to the waters with its meal.

Due to the large number of <u>visitors</u> to Loch Ness, more than <u>100,000</u> each year, observations of such a beast should be common. With sightings a rarity, some speculators believe the monster lurks in the depths feeding on <u>plankton</u>, perhaps in the form of a <u>giant squid</u>. However, large quantities of plankton needed to sustain such a large creature only live near the surface of the lake.

Perhaps, according to one <u>hypothesis</u>, the monster is a <u>rare</u> form of <u>giant eel</u>. Several members of the eel family live at the bottom of water <u>feeding</u> at the surface only <u>at night</u>.

More likely, the water kelpie is only a shadowy <u>conglomerate</u> of stories told for hundreds of years around the glow of a campfire. Perhaps the monster of Loch Ness is nothing more than <u>primeval</u> memory of dark, liquid demons and imaginary phantoms dancing in the mist of decaying peat.

Source: Reading Stories for Comprehension Success: Intermediate Level, Grades 4–6 by Katherine Hall (Jossey-Bass, San Francisco, 1996).

2. Create a CUE CARD to illustrate target highlighting. Often, students forget that they can highlight text as they read. They are aware of its benefits, but do not initiate its use without a reminder. Feel free to copy the following illustration for students' desks or enlarge it for a bulletin board. The instructor could merely point to the bulletin board as a reminder for all to use highlighting.

◗ Strategy 3-4: Quickie Study List from Highlighted Text "list it"

Observed Behavior

Jeremy took his books home to study for the test. He read his notes and re-scanned his highlighted text. His mother quizzed him on the facts as she saw them, and Jeremy performed quite well. However, when Jeremy took the test at school, he had a hard time remembering some of the specific new details, especially the new vocabulary terms. He remembered them immediately after he had "studied" them at home in his mother's test, but he couldn't remember the new vocabulary the next day.

Jeremy did everything he knew how to do to study for the test, yet he had trouble recalling new details on the day of his test. This problem is called *delayed recall*. When some students practice hard and then immediately are tested, they perform well; but given a time delay between studying and testing, they lose some of the new—or complex—information. Remember, if students are to be able to recall it easily, new information must be "hooked to" old knowledge to fix it permanently into their long-term memory, or memory "storehouse." Although his mother did test him on the facts as *she* saw them, Jeremy had not personally chosen the specific study facts in a way that had meaning for him. Only the students themselves know what is new or still confusing. Students benefit from the use of tools that put extra emphasis on identifying the "new stuff." A special study tool might provide Jeremy with a means of describing the meaning of the new terminology. So, how does Jeremy create a study list to identify terms that need extra work to become etched solidly into his memory, so he can remember them the next day?

Strategies and Tools to Improve the Student's Performance

Jeremy needs a tool that will let him list his personal choices of difficult terms that need study. If he has highlighted his text, he's halfway to creating a vertical study list.

To create this list, the instructor needs to provide a visual layout. (A sample is included at the end of this strategy section.) Start with a lined piece of paper folded vertically down the middle. Next, instruct Jeremy to select specific words from his highlighting that he personally knows he must spend more time studying. Jeremy then writes these words down the left-hand side of the vertically folded paper, being careful not to write across the fold line. Each term he believes may be on the test should be written with one or two empty spaces following it. These extra spaces will be needed later to write in definitions on the opposite side of the paper. (Students have stated that they sometimes have difficulty because the writing on the back "bleeds" through to the front, so, for reading clarity, they prefer to use a separate sheet of paper.) When the list fills the left side of the page, a new page is begun.

Once his list is complete, Jeremy can re-scan his list and decide which terms are weak. Most students know when they "know" something. Only if they don't know what a fact word means should they re-scan the highlighted text to find it and write a short, paraphrased description. Students can be taught how to note key words hidden in new terminology and use the key words to create associations and write sentences about the new words' meanings. (This skill is more fully explored later in the last memory strategy.) The meanings or associations will be written on the right side of the fold directly across from the fact word. Some students also enjoy illustrating their definitions and associations.

1. Use the recipe that follows to create a "study list."

- Instruct students to vertically fold a piece of lined paper.

- Write the topic that is being explored.

- Write the label "facts" at the top of the left side of the paper.

- Write the label "information or definition" at the top of the right side.

- Instruct students to re-scan highlighted text and locate study words or phrases that require additional study.

- Write each fact word on a line on the left side and skip down one or two spaces.

- Remind the students that they should *not* write on the back of the paper.

- Complete the entire list of fact words needing study.

- Go back to the top of the list and add *paraphrased* definitions where needed.

- Create associations with key words for new terminology when helpful.

- Illustrate the associations (individual choice).

Why does a study list improve memory? The vertical study list tool builds stronger memory for new information by increasing attention and concentration on the identification of words that need study. The students' attempts to paraphrase the definition of the word instead of simply copying it from the book force them to think about how this new word is like other words they already know. This hooking together of old and new information creates a clearer path for re-finding the new term at the time of the test. In addition, the process of writing adds another source of memory—motor memory. Finally, students who are skilled with visualization or mental imaging may be able to recapture a mental picture of the meaning as they imagined it. They may also be able to re-visualize the printed word in its actual position on the page and see the printed word in their mind. All of these memory sources are tapped when the students make a vertical study list. Therefore, and most important, Jeremy can quickly review by studying with his vertical study list, and may improve his delayed recall of new information.

Here is a sample study list based on highlighted text from the previous strategy.

STUDY LIST FOR: *Monster in the Loch*	
facts	**information or definition**
conjure	*think hard to see or imagine*
Loch Ness	*lake in Scotland* *23mi - 754 ft deep - 42°F*
Celtic myths	*legends of Scottish, Irish*
kelpies	*water monster lives in "kelp" head "horse shape" horse eels*
tentacula	*raised ears/horns*
plesiosaurs	*dino. age marine reptiles*
mr/mrs Spices	*sighting 1933*
lumbering	*walk heavy - legs like "lumber"*
peat	*decaying plant matter*
primeval	*relates to early/ancient time*

2. Teach students to test themselves using their own list. When the vertical study list with added descriptions is complete, students can then test themselves by folding the answers under so they are not exposed while the students attempt to describe them. This self-testing could be performed using these two techniques:

- Fold under the definitions to test students' ability to describe the terms. With this technique, the students read the word and attempt to recite (aloud) the meaning.

- Reverse the procedure. Ask students to look at the definition and identify the specific term. This is harder because it is more difficult to find, or retrieve, specific words in our memory by reading their meaning. As a result, it is suggested that the reverse procedure of hiding the specific words be done after students are familiar with the terms. However, when studying with this tool, the students can simply uncover the answer to re-see it, thus possibly strengthening their ability to recall it during a test.

- <u>Added idea:</u> If the students remain unable to recall certain terms, they could star (*) the difficult items in the left-hand margin of the paper and review the following morning before taking the test.

3. Create a CUE CARD to illustrate a vertical study list. Some students need reminders to make a study list. The entire class could be asked to write a vertical study list. Students could be provided with a pre-folded "study list" sheet to be placed in their book as a home-reminder. Yet, in the classroom, they may still not initiate its use without a specific reminder. The following CUE CARD can be copied or enlarged and placed in texts, on desks, or on bulletin boards.

Strategy 3-5: Draw Meaning Illustrations for Vocabulary   "draw it"

Observed Behavior

Carol's assignment is to study her new vocabulary list for a test. Following her teacher's suggestions, she copies the words in a list and writes the definitions. She even uses the definition phrases in simple sentences. She re-reads the list and rehearses the definitions, but still has difficulty recalling half of the new words' meanings on her practice test with her father. At breakfast, Carol reviews the hard word meanings in the sentences with her father. But on the test, she remembers only 70 percent of the words' meanings. All her hard effort didn't pay off and she is becoming discouraged.

Carol has followed all her teacher's suggestions about how to study. She's even expanded on them by getting her father's help with reviewing difficult items at a time closer to the actual test. Why is she continuing to encounter difficulty? Her teacher knows that Carol is a bright student, so ability is not what is limiting her success. An instructor's closer look at the sentences Carol has created reveals that Carol's interpretations of the words' meanings are literal. Students' use of literal interpretations is not unusual. Most students use dictionaries or text meanings that are phrase descriptions rather than complete sentence descriptions. Carol had merely copied the definition phrases from her book into a sentence that contained no further context description that was meaningful to her. As a result, Carol was simply memorizing the definition words without truly understanding their meanings. She had not related the word meaning to anything she had experienced. Without experiencing the word's meaning, she could not imagine how it looked in real life. So, all her practice with verbal-memory strategies did not build a strong enough memory path in her brain to enable her to recall them later during the test.

Strategies and Tools to Improve the Student's Performance

What if Carol were encouraged to explore visual strategies instead of words alone? What if she actually learned better when she could see or visualize the meaning of a word? She could supplement her study techniques with visual techniques for the more challenging words on her list. Remember, she did recall 70 percent of the items with her verbal strategies, so she would only need to use visual strategies on the hard-to-remember items. Of course, she could use visual strategies for all the words on her word list, but because her teacher required the verbal strategies in the written assignment, this would probably be excessive. Also, Carol probably instinctively knows which terms are really hard for her, so she'll know which terms need extra work.

1. Teach students to "draw it." The most basic of visual strategies for improving memory is to create a visual illustration, or drawing, for the meaning of a word. To do this, a student must have enough information about the word to be able to imagine what it would look like (noun/adjective) or what it would act like (verb/adverb). Information about new word meanings can be developed in group activities by describing specific experiences in which the word meaning was encountered, such as viewing movie or video clips, cutting out magazine illustrations for meanings, acting out the meanings of words, or drawing illustrations.

Now when Carol completes her vocabulary study list, she adds illustrations next to the words that were difficult to remember on her practice test. You will notice that her illustrations represent either an action or an object. She also adds parts of speech labels (N = noun, V = verb, A = adjective).

Here is Carol's completed "draw it" sample (conform, gorge, ignite, slither).

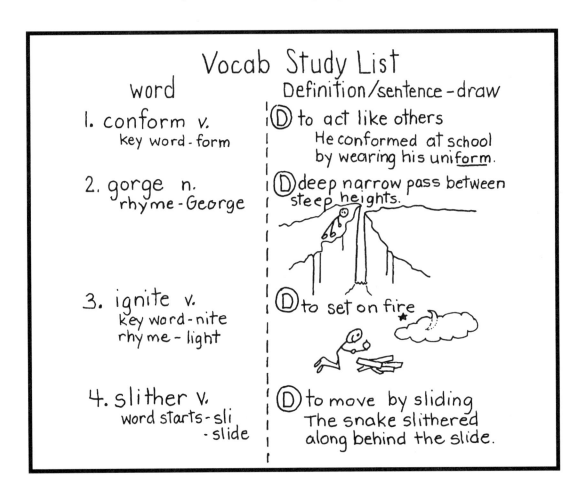

2. Create a set of vocabulary study cards. Write vocabulary words on the front side of cards. On the back of each card, the students can write an expanded definition sentence and/or a drawing of the meaning. The instructor can make a set of cards for classroom use as an enrichment activity. Students might also volunteer or rotate the responsibility of creating the vocabulary cards for extra credit. The activity could be set aside on a table at the back of the room as a "Bonus Credit" activity that could be completed in a student's spare time.

3. Follow the instructions below to teach the use of vocabulary cards. Vocabulary cards can increase memory even more if the student is shown two ways to practice with the cards. **Say:**

"First, lay out all cards with the vocabulary words facing up. See how many you can describe accurately. Turn over the card to see how you did. Which ones did you find challenging?"

"Second, lay out the cards with the definitions or illustrations facing up. See if you can name the vocabulary word. Turn over the card to see how you did. Which ones were challenging?"

"Finally, keep track of the items you have difficulty recalling. These are the ones you need to practice more."

4. Create CUE CARDS to illustrate the "draw it" strategy. Students with good visual memories should be reminded to "draw it." Even though the use of drawing may be very successful for them, they may forget to activate its use while they are studying. The following CUE CARD for the "draw it" strategy could be attached to a desk, placed on a text cover, or taken home and placed in a study area.

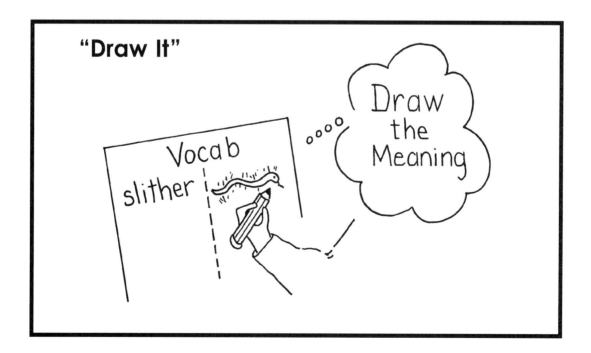

Worksheet

Vocabulary Study List

Following is a layout sheet for creating a vocabulary study list. It is meant as a convenience for the instructor; however, it is also intended to provide students with a more organized system for study that includes drawing options. If students consistently work with the same layout, they tend to automatically include drawing in their "thinking."

Name_____ **Date**_____

Vocabulary Study List

word and part of speech   definition
key words   sentence and/or draw

1.	

Strategy 3-6: Word Shape Boxes for Reading and Spelling "word boxes"

Observed Behavior

Arthur is trying to read his new sight words to his teacher. Each word is written on an index card. Although Arthur knows a majority of the letter sounds for the first letters of words, he cannot say all the sounds in the word in exact order and blend them to figure out the words. Often he does not say the sounds in the order in which they are written within the word. He constantly needs to turn over the cards to see the illustration for the word to know what it is.

Arthur is not mastering his sight vocabulary words for beginning reading. He is having difficulty doing this task that requires noticing the order or sequence of printed letter symbols. Although he can pronounce most of the first-position letter sounds, he misorders the sounds for the letters in the middle of the words. Even when he can pronounce the sounds in order correctly, he cannot blend the sounds to recognize the whole word. This behavior indicates Arthur is having difficulty with tasks that require him to sequence and blend individual letters and their sounds. He is obviously frustrated when he is attempting to use verbal, or auditory, memory skills. Could there be another way to help Arthur learn new words?

Strategies and Tools to Improve the Student's Performance

Arthur may be able to use his visual memory to build a working sight vocabulary for beginning reading. We need to help him use his visual, or seeing, skills. Using visual memory requires students to see the whole word at one time. Words for Arthur must appear as a single unit, so his word cards should be changed. We need to draw a line that exactly traces around the external edge, or *configuration*, of each word. This configuration of a word is also called a "word box." Now when Arthur looks at his cards, he will see that each word has a specific shape.

1. Use sight word boxes for the visual configuration of words. Some samples are shown on page 151. The word boxes alone would probably not maximize Arthur's potential for using his visual memory. Words learned on cards are printed without a line under them. The words may appear to the new learner as if they are floating in space. The words are not grounded to show where the actual letters sit on the line of print. Remember, some letters hang down or stick up tall, changing the shape of words. Worst of all, words are often introduced on a flat table surface or printed on unlined paper, so letters are not analyzed from a standing position. The significance of the line on which we place letters and words is never explained to students.

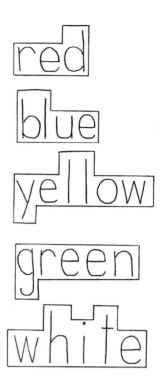

For the potential visual learner, it is essential to understand the visual spatial significance of where a word sits in space and its relationship to nearby words. Arthur must be able to visually compare and contrast word box shapes to be able to distinguish which one is which. Without these skills, visual learners cannot maximize the use of word boxes for mastering reading words. Arthur must understand how words and the individual letters sit in relation to a line of print and where the front and back of the word should be.

2. **Provide concrete demonstrations for critical visual skills.**

- Individual letter stroke parts and order of parts (See Section 2, Attention-Enhancing Strategies.)
- Individual position of letters as standing on a line (grounding position)
- Individual word position as standing on a line
- Individual word position from the front or starting point
- Individual word position where it ends
- Individual word height and depth (above and below the line or "ground")
- Individual word length for visual comparison
- Individual letter sounds vs. double letter sounds (**th, ch, sh, wh, ph,** and **ng**) (See Section 4, Organization-Enhancing Strategies.)

Initially Arthur would benefit from actually seeing his words displayed on a vertical surface, not on a flat table, desk, or paper. Using a magnetic board with a "ground" line drawn on it, letters in words could be more accurately analyzed in their "standing" position on the line. As the letters for words are placed on the ground line, the instructor should point out that some of the letters stick up high and some hang down below the "ground" line.

The instructor can also compare the letters to houses. All letters, like houses, must sit in a specific position related to the ground. Most letters sit on the ground line, but some letters hang down below the ground. They can be seen as hanging down into the house's basement. Also, some letters are tall or short. When letters are placed in their correct position on a line to create words, the "roof" lines and "basement" lines vary, depending on the specific letters included in the word. Students could improve whole word learning if they understood the visual differences of the position of letters on the line. Thus, each word "house," created by drawing a line around the word, has a different external shape, or configuration.

3. Teach visual word learners by breaking down letter shapes by their positions on the ground line.

- "Short" letters that extend up only half a space: a, c, e, m, n, o, r, s, u, v, w, x, z
- "Stick up" letters that extend up to the full space: b, d, f, h, k, l, t
- "Hang down" letters that extend down below the ground line: g, p, q, y
- "Short dot" letter that extends above the halfway space: i
- "Hang down dot" letter that extends above the halfway and below the ground: j

4. Build words with paper letter models. Once students have experimented with building words with three-dimensional letters on a standing surface, they are ready to build the words on a flat surface. To provide practice with interpreting words on a flat surface, students can be given paper models for the letters that have a "ground" line included in each letter. New sight words could be copied by placing the paper model letters in order, carefully matching the ground lines on each letter. A full set of paper models for lowercase letters appears at the end of this strategy. They can be copied and laminated for your use with students. Be sure to include the ground line in the "letter boxes" when they are cut.

Here are sample sight words created with paper letter models with "ground" lines attached.

After the students have played with the individual letter boxes to create words on a flat table surface, they are ready to draw their own "word boxes." A word box is drawn starting on the far left side of the word on the ground line. A start mark, or dot, in the correct start position on the ground line will help the student know where to begin the drawing to create a word house. Additional samples of worksheets for practicing the drawing of word houses are included at the end of this section.

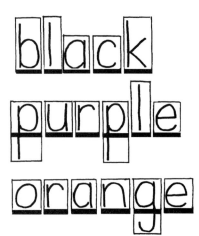

5. Before students complete the worksheets, use the following sample task to model how to draw word houses.

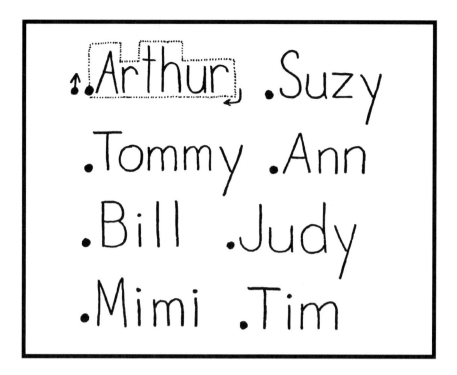

As students draw more houses, they will begin to notice general differences in the external shapes. Some students don't independently compare word differences, so they would benefit from instruction on how to note differences. To improve the students' ability to analyze and compare whole word shapes, the instructor could point out the following general variables in word houses. (Sample worksheets for further practice are at the end of this strategy.)

- Roof lines can be flat or sticking up at the front or back of a word.

    come . . . . vs. foam

    bone . . . . vs. coat

- Basement lines can hang down at the front or ends of words.

    gum . . . . vs. mug

- Front and back doors can be short or tall and above or below ground.

    hello . . . . . . vs. pat

- Length of words can be short or long.

    run . . . . . . vs. runner

Flat Roof: come

Stick-up Roofs:

foam   coat

Basements:

mug   gum

Front & Back Doors:

hello   roll

Short & Long House

run   runner

6. Create CUE CARDS to illustrate the "word house" strategy. Even though Arthur may have mastered the concepts for word houses, he may forget to use these tools to check words he finds confusing. He may benefit from having a CUE CARD placed on his desk to remind him to use the strategy.

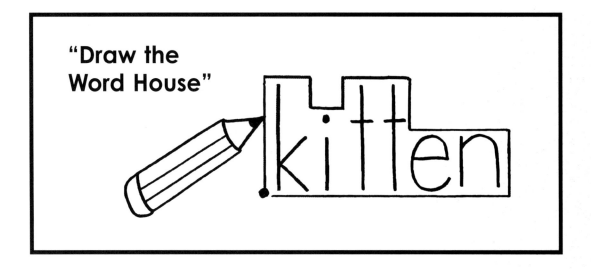

Worksheets

Letter Models with Ground Lines

Following are individual letter boxes for each letter of the alphabet. Each letter box has a "ground" line included within it. When cutting each box, be very careful to include the ground line.

Note: You can use the letter boxes to demonstrate the position of letters on a line. You might also give students their own set of letter boxes to make words that show the position of letters inside words.

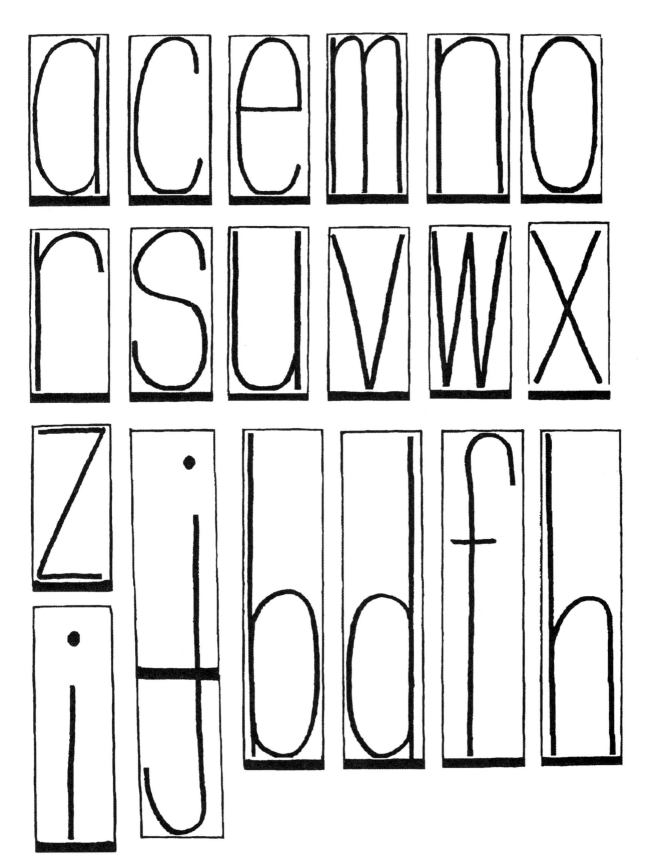

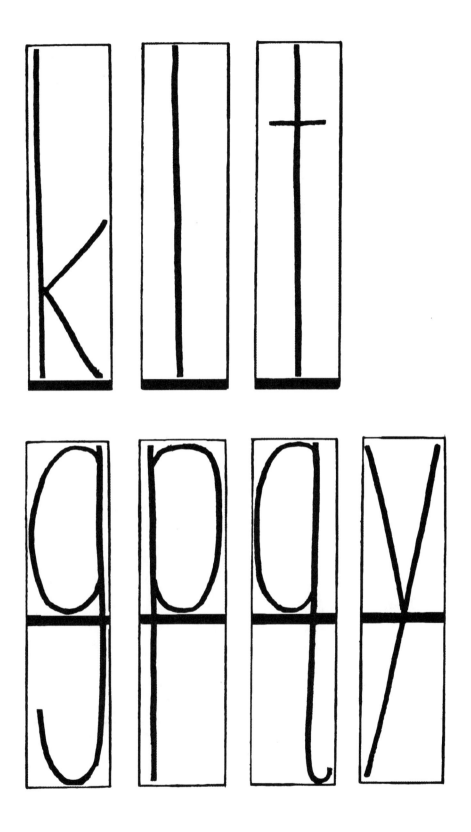

Worksheets

Practice with Comparing Word Houses

- Drawing Word Houses—1
- Drawing Word Houses—2
- Drawing Word Houses—3

Drawing Word Houses—1

Directions: 1. Draw a line around the word shape.
2. Make an X on the word that is not the same.

1. see	see	set
2. beef	bean	bean
3. clock	click	clock
4. went	wait	wait
5. soak	sick	soak
6. pane	pane	mane
7. kick	king	kick
8. path	bath	bath
9. best	nest	best
10. cold	gold	gold
11. tack	talk	tack

number correct: ___/10

Drawing Word Houses—2

Directions: 1. Draw a line around the word shape.
2. Make an X on the word that is not the same.

1.	land	lane	land
2.	hug	hug	bun
3.	pack	pack	back
4.	undo	do	do
5.	shake	snake	snake
6.	bath	bang	bang
7.	pear	bear	bear
8.	run	run	run
9.	belt	unbelt	belt
10.	clock	clink	clink
11.	match	matches	match

number correct: ___/10

Drawing Word Houses—3

Directions: 1. Draw a line around the word shape.
2. Make an X on the word that is not the same.

1.	make	make	mane
2.	boat	boar	boat
3.	yell	yell	tell
4.	soap	soak	soap
5.	lock	block	block
6.	poor	door	poor
7.	long	long	gong
8.	lamp	camp	camp
9.	look	like	look
10.	clock	click	click
11.	hide	hide	ride

number correct: ___/10

Strategy 3-7: Previewing Illustrations to Predict Reading Content   "preview it . . . the picture"

Observed Behavior

Ade is struggling through her turn at reading the new story in her reading group. Each time she encounters a difficult word, she immediately attempts to "sound out" the word. Often she can't remember the sounds she has made for letters by the time she gets to the end of the word, so she can't blend the sounds together to produce a recognizable whole word. When her attempts to do so fail, she pauses to look at the illustration at the top of the page. If the difficult word is near the end of a sentence she has been able to read, her quick scan at the illustration appears to help her "guess" the difficult word. Usually, however, she is very dependent upon the teacher to tell her the word, so she can continue reading.

Ade is obviously having difficulty with sequencing letter sounds to "figure out" unrecognizable words while reading stories. She is not able to use auditory memory skills for decoding with individual letter sounds. This does not mean to imply that the instructor should completely stop instruction on how to decode words by using letter sound skills. All students must eventually learn how the sound "code" for letters works in decoding words, because there are moments when they will be forced to use them at least partially.

Yet, for the present, Ade might be able to use the visual illustrations in stories to improve her accuracy in "guessing" words while reading. As a probable visual learner, Ade sneaks a peek at the illustration to get clues about what the unknown printed word might be in the sentence. To more effectively use the illustrations, she would benefit from direct instruction on how, by previewing illustrations prior to reading, she can predict or anticipate the content of a written story.

Strategies and Tools to Improve the Student's Performance

How could emphasizing story illustrations improve Ade's word decoding? Each spoken or printed word in our language has a matching visual image for meaning. Verbal learners go into their "word storehouse" to discover what the word is. However, visual learners more naturally go into their "picture storehouse" to recognize what it could be. So for Ade, the illustrations at the tops of pages or contained with the text of the story become a source of knowledge. These illustrations actually forecast what word labels might be used in the printed story. The saying "a picture is worth a thousand words" further explains this skill that visual learners personally understand. In the process of visually looking at an illustration, the brain is making connections between the pictured items and the words that will match them. By encouraging Ade to take time to think what the story might be about from the illustration, her brain has time to make those connections and predict probable ideas and word labels that logically might be used in the upcoming story.

So, how do we teach Ade to capitalize on her visual skill for using illustrations to improve her word decoding difficulties?

First, encourage her to carefully examine the illustration, not just sneak a peek at it. She must clearly understand that it is wise to look at the pictures, not a sign of weakness.

Second, teach her how to systematically look at all the details in the illustrations so she does not overlook anything important. Remember, visual learners tend to see the whole idea or the general theme. They do not naturally examine details in a systematic or sequential process, so they often overlook small details.

Third, teach Ade to independently preview illustrations prior to reading, so she can call on her "predicted" word labels as she needs them while reading. She will likely need reminders initially to remember to carefully examine illustrations to help her predict or anticipate story content.

1. Use the recipe below to instruct students about predicting content from story illustrations. Select a group of probable visual learners who would benefit from learning this strategy. Demonstrate "previewing illustrations" with their next story reading.

- Instruct students to specifically look at the illustration for the page before reading.
- Explain to students why they are going to preview the story before reading it.
  - Use terms they understand, for example: "We can sometimes read and understand better when we know what the story is about." OR "We can sometimes read better when we know what is going to happen in the story."
- Tell the students they are going to learn a way to look more carefully at pictures, so they can read better. Model how:
  - Move a pointing finger across the picture to note details.
  - Talk aloud as the picture is examined.
- Based on the picture they are looking at, ask:
  - "Could you make 'guesses' about what might happen in the story?"
  - "Could you make 'guesses' about what the story might be about?"

▶ Write their "guesses" on a paper, so they can later see if their predictions were correct.

● Model the reading of a page, looking back at the picture for word clues or story event clues.

● After reading a page, ask:

▶ "What things in the picture helped with word reading or knowing what was coming?"

▶ "What was not included that you could add to the picture?" (*Optional*: Draw it.)

● Repeat the procedure for previewing an illustration prior to reading each page.

● For the next story, have students in the group take turns describing:

▶ What they see in the picture.

▶ What they predict might happen in the next part.

2. Have students complete the sample activity on page 165 to practice previewing the pictures. Remind students to carefully analyze the illustration first and then to read the story.

For the Love of Patty Cake

In 1972, a baby gorilla named Patty Cake was born at New York's Central Park Zoo. Patty Cake's parents, Lulu and Kongo, loved their baby very much. They hugged Patty Cake and played with her.

The Central Park Zoo was very old. It had old box cages with heavy bars. One day while playing with Lulu, Patty Cake broke her arm on the bars.

The arm was put in a cast. The zoo keeper called the newer Bronx Zoo. He asked them to keep Patty Cake until her arm was better. Lulu or Kongo might take off the cast, and hurt Patty Cake's arm again.

Patty Cake got better fast. When it was time to go home, the Bronx Zoo wanted to keep her. They said the old cage was dangerous.

The Central Park Zoo asked Ronald D. Nadler, who studied gorillas, for help. He told the Bronx Zoo that Patty Cake needed her family. He told the Central Park Zoo to make safer cages.

After three months, Patty Cake went home to Lulu and Kongo. The family was happy to be together at last.

Source: *Reading Stories for Comprehension Success: Intermediate Level, Grades 4–6* by Katherine Hall (Jossey-Bass, San Francisco, 1996).

Even though this strategy is very effective for visual learners, struggling students do not automatically preview illustrations on each page just prior to reading. As a result, they need reminders, such as CUE CARDS.

3. Create CUE CARDS for the "previewing illustrations" strategy. A CUE CARD could be placed at the top edge of students' desks as a visual reminder. The instructor could also enlarge the following CUE CARD and place it on a bulletin board so that the entire class is reminded to use previewing of illustrations. The instructor could merely point to the CUE CARD with a verbal announcement of "Don't forget to . . ."

Strategy 3-8: Previewing Content in Chapter Reading "preview it"

Observed Behavior

Ming can read at grade level, but his science text contains many above-grade-level words and specialized scientific terms that are hard for him to figure out. Therefore, he often struggles to even finish reading a chapter.

It's not unusual for students to encounter reading problems when they begin chapter reading in specific areas of content. Textbooks at a chapter level are designed to include new and specialized terms, which can be large, multisyllabic words that are more difficult to "figure out" or decode. As a result, students who struggle with decoding find that reading the text will be difficult for them. They are almost prepared to be frustrated before they even begin. How do we help them face this difficult task, so they can actually get information from the text?

Strategies and Tools to Improve the Student's Performance

Luckily, Ming is skilled at using pictures to help understand concepts that are expressed in words. Remember, the rule for visual learners is "a picture is worth a thousand words." Let's show him how to use the pictures in the text to get an overview of the text ideas before he begins to read. When he has a better sense of what is in the chapter, Ming will be better prepared to reach conclusions about the chapter's content. Given a visual prediction, Ming's brain will be more equipped to recognize words instead of being forced to "figure out" each new word.

This process of analyzing visual information with limited inspection of the words is called *previewing* or *scanning*. We must show Ming how to scan the headings, illustrations, and bold printed words in the chapter before actually attempting to read the text. Chapter scanning should also include the reading of the end-of-chapter, or unit, questions. While reading the questions, Ming should be encouraged to try and "guess" the answers to the questions and possibly attempt to figure out where the answer would be located in the text. Luckily, the questions often contain words included in the headings. After completing his preview, he would be more likely to recognize the heading words, which would in turn give him clues about where to find the answers to the questions. Only after completing a chapter preview would Ming begin his actual reading. Having gained a general sense of the main ideas and a preview of the new vocabulary, he would be better able to read the chapter and better understand the concepts. Given the time needed to preview a chapter, this skill is ideally practiced at home. Parents could be sent a copy of the instruction recipe, which is included below, so they could demonstrate the skill and assist their child in perfecting its use.

In addition, because the difficult-to-decode and complex words for specialized terminology are often required for curriculum mastery, his teacher would have to discuss these terms more thoroughly with the class. With the teacher's discussion of the difficult-to-read words and Ming's practice in previewing, his frustration with word decoding could be reduced. Ming would undoubtedly have more confidence in his chapter reading.

1. Use the following recipe to instruct students about chapter previewing. Students learn best by watching someone actually doing a preview. The modeling should include pointing, self-questioning aloud, and pausing to think.

- Compare the new chapter to the last chapter.
  - ▶ It is important to "hook" the past knowledge to the new information to ensure that everything fits together. Ideas "hooked" together in this fashion are easier to remember. The student could ask, "What does this new chapter have to do with the chapter I just finished?"
- Check out the "key word box."
  - ▶ The student could ask, "Do I recognize any of the words? Do I know what any of the words mean?"
- Scan the first section for headings, bold printed words, and nearby illustrations.
  - ▶ The student could ask, "What does this heading have to do with the chapter title? How are the illustrations connected to the heading? Are there any bold printed words in the section? What could they mean? Maybe I'll read just the sentence around the bold word for clues about what it means."
- Repeat the procedure for all sections by scanning the headings, bold words, and illustrations.
- Read the end-of-unit or chapter questions and identify possible words that may be "heading words." Look for heading words in the text to help find answers. (Many students find it helpful to read the review questions first.)
- Finally, read the text, but remember to use highlighting if it helps you remember.

2. Assist the students in chapter previewing.

- Sit with the students and encourage them to make guesses about what is seen. Remind them that there are no right answers. It's just a preview to get an idea of what the chapter might be saying. Ask the students to talk it aloud, so you can hear their good ideas.

● Complete the chapter preview and assist in the question-reading step. Point out to students that some of the questions will be easy after a preview, but some will need more real reading. If they are interested, help them find where they think the answer might be located in the chapter. Remember, questions usually contain "heading words" that help us find the answer easier.

3. Use chapter previewing as homework. Copy the above "recipe" and the "assisting the student" description. Send these home as a homework assignment. Attach a note for parents suggesting that it would be helpful if they could assist their child in performing the previewing of the assigned chapter or unit.

4. Create CUE CARDS to illustrate chapter previewing. Reminders may be necessary to encourage the student to do a preview. Once this strategy of previewing is practiced and actually seen as valuable, students will want to use it. Yet, given the load of homework, students are rushing so fast they may forget. So the following CUE CARD can be placed on the desk or on the text or enlarged to use on a bulletin board as a visual reminder to use previewing.

➤ Strategy 3-9: Double-Digit Number Reading for Reversals   "talk the numbers"

Observed Behavior

As the teacher dictates the adding problems, Nita is writing the numbers on her paper. She is grimacing as she looks at her numbers. She is not sure if they are right, so she glances at the classroom number chart to check them. However, she is still making mistakes. Many of the double-digit numbers are reversed in their order on her paper. That same grimacing expression appears when she writes page numbers for assignments.

Nita is not unusual in having difficulty with visually interpreting double-digit numbers. Many students are confused with both reading and writing numbers. Nita has learned the individual number digits, but somehow she has not mastered the global concept that all multidigit numbers must be read from left to right. Her teacher reports that Nita has reviewed this concept, but she continues to make mistakes in writing numbers. For example, the number 23, if read in the reverse direction, would be interpreted as 32. It is likely that Nita's visual confusion with interpreting numbers will remain a problem due to weaknesses in her visual analysis skills. So, how can we help?

Strategies and Tools to Improve the Student's Performance

Instead of continuing to frustrate Nita with visual practice in number reading, why not show her how to use her auditory, or verbal, memory skills to compensate for her visual weakness? By seeing and hearing her spoken words, she may be able to better interpret the numbers she sees. Luckily for Nita, most double-digit numbers, when they are spoken aloud, are said in the exact order they should be written or read. This rule is true for all double-digit numbers except the "teen" numbers which are "stinkers" that don't play fair. A separate strategy will be described later for the "teen" numbers.

If you listen to the spoken words for regular two-digit numbers, you can hear the correct order of digits. For example, the number 43, when said aloud, is "four" + "t" + "three." The spoken words tell the listener to write the 4 first because the

4 was said first and then write the 3 because it was said last. If Nita listens very carefully, she will also notice that she said "t" between the "four" and the "three." The letter "t" stands for the word "tens." So "four-t-three" is four tens and three ones. This concept is based on a Chinese teaching practice, used with the abacus.

We must show Nita how to use "talking the numbers" in parallel with her looking at numbers to ensure that she does not misinterpret what she sees. There are five specific skills that must be learned to master the concept of "talking numbers."

First, Nita must learn to listen to her spoken words for double-digit numbers.

Second, Nita must see the "spoken words rule" applied to all the numbers from one to one hundred. A grid, or hundred-box graph, with the numbers written in rows of tens should be visible for comparing the spoken number to the printed numbers. The concept of increasing rows of tens is clarified by using a new color to write each row of numbers in the hundreds grid.

Third, Nita needs to learn that the "talking" of numbers does not always sound exactly like it should, but it is close enough to recognize what the number should be. For example, when she hears the spoken "twen" it means twenties or two. She will need to learn that a spoken "thir" means thirties or a three, and a spoken "fif" means fifties or a five.

Fourth, Nita needs to learn that all the other digits are spoken with the correct number words. For example, the "six" for sixties, "seven" for seventies, "eight" for eighties, and "nine" for nineties.

Finally, Nita must learn that the concept of "teen" numbers does not follow the "talking" rule. (This will be explored separately.)

Double-Digit Numbers That Follow the Talking Rule

1. Use the following recipe to instruct students about "talking" double-digit numbers (excluding the teens until later).

- Tell the students they are going to learn a strategy for "talking" the numbers aloud, so they can *read double-digit numbers* from 1–100. Tell students they will need to carefully listen to their own "talking" so they can hear themselves correctly.

- Explain that the "teen" numbers don't play fair, so they will be discussed later.

- Starting with the twenties, explain that when you say "twen," it means you must write a 2.
  - ▶ Give the student a "twenties" number strip that is marked with a start point arrow on the left edge of the strip. Ready-to-use number strips are included at the end of this strategy section.
  - ▶ Model the spoken words for the "twenties" while touching each digit in left-to-right order.

- Demonstrate how we can hear a "t" in the middle when we say the "twenties."
  - ▶ Say one of the "twenty" numbers, such as "twen-t-three."
  - ▶ Ask, "Did you hear the 'twen' first?" "Did you hear the 't' next?" "What did you hear last?"
  - ▶ Tell students they will always hear the "t" after they say the "twen."
  - ▶ Try saying some other "twenty-numbers" to see if the "t" is said in the middle.

- Illustrate the meaning of the spoken "t," or ten, with counting cubes for some of the twenties.
  - ▶ Choose a spoken number and gather a set of cubes to match its value.
  - ▶ Ask a student to find the sets of tens hiding in the pile of cubes.
  - ▶ Students benefit by seeing sets of cubes sorted into tens and ones. For example, "twen-t-three" = 23 pieces = 2 stacks of ten with 3 single cubes. Students can then see the first spoken digit always has more value.
  - ▶ Ask, "How many 'tens' were there in 23?" "Yes, 'twen' = 2 tens."

- Ask the students to repeat your modeling of "talking the numbers" as the numbers are touched on the number strips.
  - ▶ Ask for numbers in order and out of order.

- Repeat the procedure for the "thir"-ties, forties, and "fif"-ties to ensure that the students understand that a spoken "thir" means a 3 and a "fif" means a 5.

- Demonstrate the rest of the numbers (sixties, seventies, eighties, and nineties). Say the regular word for the numbers in the tens position.

- Model the touching of random numbers on the hundreds grid while saying the spoken words for the number.

- Give the students a personal copy of a color-coded tens grid for numbers 1–100. A sample is included in this strategy section.
  - ▶ Students will need to color each row with varying colors to increase their scanning accuracy from row to row.
  - ▶ Ask the students to repeat double-digit numbers as you say them so that students can feel their mouth say the number parts in order.
  - ▶ Ask the students to find numbers on the grid.

- Tell students they are going to <u>write double-digit numbers</u> as they hear them.

  ▶ Remind them to listen for the number they hear first and write it.

  ▶ Then listen for the last number and write it.

  ▶ They should check their number writing by saying it aloud.

  ▶ Give the students their hundreds grid for support while initially learning to write numbers that are dictated.

- Demonstrate how to repeat, or rehearse, the numbers that are dictated.

  ▶ Students need to experience listening to their own voice to notice what comes out of their mouth first.

  ▶ Tell them you will say a double-digit number and they are only to repeat it aloud.

  ▶ Ask students to say what they heard first. Then ask them to say the number again and write the whole number with a pencil.

2. Create CUE CARDS to illustrate the "talking the numbers" strategy.

Even after students have mastered this new strategy for "talking the numbers," they may still forget to use it, especially when they are anxious. A visual reminder to trigger the memory of the strategy may be more helpful than verbally announcing it to the students. CUE CARDS such as the following one could be placed on the students' desks, in their math books, or on a bulletin board. The instructor could then remind the students to use the strategy by simply pointing to the CUE CARD.

How to Talk the "Teen" Numbers

Without special instruction on the "teen" numbers, students could continue to be confused with double-digit numbers because the "teen" numbers are actually said in the reverse order. For example, "fourteen" says the 4 first and the "teen" last. If you followed the "spoken words" rule, "fourteen" might be written as 4 first, then 1, or 41. The student could mistakenly apply the "spoken words" rule and reverse all the teen numbers.

To master the "teen numbers," students must learn some basic concepts.

First, students must learn to recognize when they hear the spoken word "teen" in their reading of teen numbers. It is often difficult to distinguish a "t" from a "teen," so practice in listening may be necessary. It may be helpful to point out to students that they can actually feel the "n" sound coming out of their nose when they exaggerate the spoken word "teen" as compared with the "t," which means a ten.

Second, to enable them to remember that the spoken "teen" numbers are written in the reverse of what is heard, students must create a memorable association for the word "teen." Students often appreciate the humor of thinking of teenagers as bossy, because they may have experienced bossy teenagers in their own homes or neighborhoods. Neighborhood teens are often considered the "bossy" ones by younger children. This comparison fits with the concept of teen numbers, which could be considered as bossy, because they break the rules.

Third, students must learn to recognize that the "1" digit in spoken teen numbers always comes first. Like a bossy teenager, the 1 digit would always want to be first, so it jumps in front. The 1 digit can be illustrated as a bossy teenager standing with hands on hips and a grimace on the face. (A sample illustration of the 1 digit as a bossy teenager is included later in this strategy section.)

Finally, students must carefully watch out for left-to-right direction in the order of the teen number digits. They must learn to notice that the teenager number 1 always comes first. Initially, we can make an arrow pointing from left to right in front of each "teen" number.

1. Use this recipe for instructing students about the "teen" numbers.

- Explain that they are going to learn how "teen" numbers don't play fair. The spoken words for "teens" do not follow the correct left-to-right order.

- Demonstrate how the word "teen," when spoken, has an "n," or nose sound.

    ▶ Say the word "teen" slowly, holding the "n" sound longer to feel the sound coming out of the nose.

    ▶ Ask students to repeat your spoken numbers (regular and teen numbers).

    ▶ Explain that they will hear "t" and "teen" in the numbers.

    ▶ Ask students to raise their hands when they hear a number with the spoken word "teen" in it.

- Demonstrate how the 1 digit always comes first in "teen" numbers.
  - ▶ Display a set of "teen" number cards in both a *vertical* and *horizontal* list, so students can see that the 1 digit always comes first in teens. (A sample set of "teen" cards is included in this strategy section.)
- Explain that the numbers 11 and 12 are actually teen numbers, but they don't say "teen."
  - ▶ It is often effective to point out that the person who invented numbers could have called 11 "one-teen" and 12 "two-teen."
- Model the spoken words for:
  - ▶ 13 as "thir"teen because "thir" means a 3.
  - ▶ 15 as "fif"teen because "fif" means a 5.
  - ▶ All other "teens" say the right word for the number.
- Demonstrate how to draw the visual association for the numeral 1 as a teenager with hands on hips looking very bossy. (A sample illustration is included in this strategy section.)
- Ask the students to draw the teenager on the 1 digit. (A sample worksheet is included in this strategy section.)
- On a worksheet with *only teen numbers*, ask students to draw the teenager illustration on the *first* 1 digit for the teen numbers. (A sample worksheet is included in this strategy section.)
- In two vertical columns, sort cards (teens and 21, 31, 41, 51, 61, 71, 81, 91) to show the position of the 1 digit.
  - ▶ Read the numbers while touching each digit.
  - ▶ Ask the student to read the cards in mixed order.
- On a worksheet with *mixed numbers* (both regular and teen numbers), ask students to draw the teenager illustration only on the first digit of the teen numbers.

2. Use the tools below to teach students about the "teen" numbers. Samples are included at the end of this strategy section.

- A set of cards for teen numbers and regular numbers that contain a 1 digit (teen numbers and 21, 31, 41, 51, 61, 71, 81, 91).
- A sample illustration for the teen as a bossy teenager.
- A worksheet for drawing the teen illustration.
- A worksheet with all teen numbers for students to add the teenager drawing.
- A worksheet with mixed numbers (regular and teens) for identifying the teens and adding the teenager drawing.

Although most students quickly recognize the concept of teen numbers as "bossy" or "not playing fair," memory of the concept becomes stronger when students actively participate in drawing their own "bossy teenager" illustrations. Remember, the motor process of handwriting or drawing is an additional means of putting information in the brain. Once the illustration is mastered, students should then add the drawing to actual teen numbers. Tasks with mixed sets of numbers containing both teen and regular numbers should be provided to ensure students know when to appropriately add the teenager illustration.

Here is a sample illustration of the "bossy teenager" drawing.

3. Use the following activity to demonstrate how to draw the "bossy teenager." An enlarged version appears with the worksheets at the end of this strategy.

Draw the bossy teenager.

Worksheets

Ready-to-Use Number Strips for 20s Through 90s

The following ready-to-use number strips for 20s through 90s are needed to visually demonstrate that double-digit numbers are ordered from left to right. With the number strips available, the students can "say" and "see" the number order. The students can also finger-trace the numbers as they are spoken. By combining the number strips in rows underneath each other, the entire visual concept of hundreds can be understood.

●→21	22	23	24	25	26	27	28	29	30
●→31	32	33	34	35	36	37	38	39	40
●→41	42	43	44	45	46	47	48	49	50
●→51	52	53	54	55	56	57	58	59	60

61	62	63	64	65	66	67	68	69	70
71	72	73	74	75	76	77	78	79	80
81	82	83	84	85	86	87	88	89	90
91	92	93	94	95	96	97	98	99	100

Worksheet

Ready-to-Use Hundred Number Grid

The hundreds grid for numbers 1–100 is needed to visually demonstrate the pattern that double-digit numbers create. It is more effective to color-code the hundreds grid with markers. The students could carefully trace each row with a different color.

○→1	2	3	4	5	6	7	8	9	10
○→11	12	13	14	15	16	17	18	19	20
○→21	22	23	24	25	26	27	28	29	30
○→31	32	33	34	35	36	37	38	39	40
○→41	42	43	44	45	46	47	48	49	50
○→51	52	53	54	55	56	57	58	59	60
○→61	62	63	64	65	66	67	68	69	70
○→71	72	73	74	75	76	77	78	79	80
○→81	82	83	84	85	86	87	88	89	90
○→91	92	93	94	95	96	97	98	99	100

Worksheets

Ready-to-Use Number Cards for "Teen"
and Regular Numbers

→11	→12	→13
→14	→15	→16
→17	→18	→19

→21	→31	→41
→51	→61	→71
→81	→91	

Worksheet

Drawing the "Bossy Teenager"

The following page is a ready-to-use worksheet for students' use in drawing the "bossy teenager." Mastering the use of the "bossy teenager" is very important for recognizing "teen" numbers when they are mixed with other numbers.

Draw the bossy teenager.

Worksheets

Finding the "Teen" Numbers

Two tasks are included. One task includes only teen numbers. The second task contains both teens and regular numbers.

Draw the "Bossy Teen" on each teen number.

 1   12   13

o→ 14   15   16

o→ 17   18   19

Careful. . . . Draw the bossy teen
only on the teen numbers.

○→ 16   31   71

○→ 21   14   18

○→ 15   91   13

◆▶ Strategy 3-10: Spelling Checking Through Reading Recognition

"check it like a reading word"

Observed Behavior

Mimi is a middle school student who gets A's on her spelling tests, but makes lots of spelling mistakes when she writes paragraphs. Multisyllable words can be particularly difficult. It's especially frustrating to her because she is a good reader who often recognizes that her questionable spellings look "funny," but she doesn't know how to correct them. She tries to check errors by saying the sounds in order or breaking the words into small chunks, but she still cannot make them look right. As a result, she selects words that are less difficult to spell and ends up reducing the quality of her writing.

Mimi's frustration is shared by a great majority of students. Even though she can break spoken words into smaller chunks or syllables, she has difficulty recalling irregular letter patterns that occur inside syllables. Although she is able to recognize when her written words "look funny," she can't figure out exactly what is wrong in the word. With weakness in both visual and auditory skills for spelling, she may benefit from capitalizing on her reading skills. Remember, she recognizes when the whole words "look funny," which means her visual memory word bank understands that the word is not correct—at least as a reading word. How do we teach Mimi to use her reading strengths to correct her spelling?

Strategies and Tools to Improve the Student's Performance

Teaching a student to use reading to assist with spelling involves four steps. Each step must be modeled for the students so they can see and hear the process.

First, students often find it helpful to break words into syllables. They should be encouraged to say the word slowly to hear the parts as they place a line under each separate syllable. To successfully do this, they may need a general review of one essential rule that helps visual spellers. That rule is "every syllable must have at least one vowel sound."

Second, the students need to systematically check all the areas of their questionable spelling words. It is logical to first examine words where errors would be easiest to recognize. For the visual speller, who tends to see words as wholes, only the letters at the front and end of words are even noticed. After years of drill on initial consonant blends, prefixes, and suffixes, students often recognize when these parts of words look wrong. Students should be advised to first examine the front and then the end of the word, leaving the middle until last. As they examine each area, students should ask themselves, "Does this part look right?" As each area of the word is visually examined, it is sometimes helpful to cover the remainder of the word, so they can better focus on just one part at a time. This is a personal student choice.

Third, when a specific area is identified as having an error, students need to determine what letters within that part could have alternative spellings. The students should ask, "What letters in this part could be spelled with different letters?" Most of the time, the error will be found in the vowel letters. However, irregular consonant or suffix patterns also can cause difficulty.

Finally, students need to rewrite their corrected spelling of the whole word. Without seeing the new word in printed form, they may not recognize it as a reading word. If this new word still "looks funny," other alternatives can be inserted and then rewritten as whole words until the correct word is found. Explain to the students that, although this strategy does not work 100 percent of the time, it usually will be very helpful. Sample dialogues for direct teaching of this strategy will follow the recipe of steps for this process.

1. Use this recipe to instruct students about spelling checking through reading. *Note:* The recipe below describes the steps needed to learn the strategy. The starred (✳) items describe the critical points of instruction.

- Explain to students that they are going to learn a new way to correct spelling errors by using their good memory for how words look in reading.

- Model the process for finding errors in spelling with an <u>error at the front</u>. Write a misspelled word with an error at the front. Say the word aloud and then in syllables. Point to and underline each syllable as it is spoken.

  ▶ Review the "one vowel per syllable" rule if needed.

  ▶ Sample words: pesefully, prefection, hachet, adress, pulite

✳ **Say:** "You are going to check the front and the end of the word first. Save the middle part until last, because it is the hardest to check."

  ▶ "Cover up parts of the word you are not checking so you can see one syllable at a time."

  ▶ "Find the part that 'looks' wrong."

✳ Model the correction of the error part with talking aloud, so students can hear the process.

  ▶ Identify which letters might be spelled with different letters.

  ▶ Rewrite the entire word with the alternative letters to show that it looks right.

  ▶ See the sample dialogue following this recipe.

❋ Repeat the process with the four remaining sample words that contain front-of-word errors.

● Write a misspelled word with an <u>error at the end</u>.

▶ Sample words: resistence, ventrical, reguler, enclozure, favorit

● Repeat the three starred steps listed above.

▶ Check the front, end, and the middle to locate the error.

▶ See the sample dialogue for errors at the end following this step-by-step listing.

● Write a misspelled word with an <u>error at the middle</u>.

▶ Sample words: repeted, tutering, sacrafice, vegitation, restraned

● Repeat the three starred steps listed above.

▶ Check the front, end, and the middle to locate the error.

▶ See the sample dialogue for errors in the middle following this step-by-step listing.

2. Use these sample dialogues to demonstrate spelling-error recognition.

Dialogue for modeling the examination of a word with an <u>error at the front</u>:

● **Say:** "We know this word **lojical** has an error, but we need to know where the error is located. Let's say it slowly to hear the parts—**loj-i-cal**. I can hear three parts. I'll just make a line under each of the three parts. Now let's check the front part. Okay, **loj** looks funny, but let's check the other parts first. The end part **cal** looks right. Now let's check the middle part. The single letter **i** is right. So it must be the first part. What letter in **loj** could be spelled with a different letter? I know it could be the **g** in the place of **j**, because they can have the same sound. I'll put **g** in its place. Let's write it—**logical**. How does it look as a reading word? That's it!"

Dialogue for modeling the examination of a word with an <u>error at the end</u>:

● **Say:** "We know this word **resistence** has an error, but we need to know where the error is located. Let's say it slowly to hear the parts—**re-sist-ence**. I can hear three parts. I'll just make a line under each of the three parts. Now, let's check the front part first. **Re** looks right. I think it is the prefix **re**. Now let's check the end part: **ence** could be right or wrong. I'm not sure, so let's look at the middle to be sure: **sist** is right especially when you put it together with **re** to make **resist**. I know that's the root word meaning. So the ending syllable must be wrong. What letter in **ence** could be spelled with a different letter? I know vowels are sometimes spelled with different letters, so maybe the **e** could be another vowel. I'll put an **a** in its place. Let's write it to see if it looks right. **Resistance** . . . that's it!"

Dialogue for modeling the examination of a word with an <u>error in the middle</u>:

- **Say:** "We know the word **repeted** has an error, but we need to know where the error is located. Let's say it slowly first to hear the parts— **re-pet-ed**. I can hear three parts. I'll just make a line under each of the three parts. Now let's check the front part first: **re** looks right because it is a prefix. Now let's check the end part: **ed** looks right because it is a suffix. So it must be the middle part. What letter in **pet** could be spelled with different letters? I know it looks funny because **pet** says PET, which is an animal and this word does not sound like **pet**. So, it must be the vowel. Oh, I see the **e** sound could be spelled as **ee** or **ea**. But I know the prefix **re** plus **peat** looks like the right word, not **re** plus **peet**. Let's write it—**repeated**. That's it!"

<u>When all else fails:</u> Remind the students to underline their spelling error words, so they will remember to come back later and ask for help when someone is available.

Most important, many students forget to use this strategy when they are in the process of writing paragraphs, so they will need gentle reminders to activate its use.

3. Create CUE CARDS to illustrate the strategy of spelling checking through reading recognition. It may be helpful to attach the CUE CARDS on their desks as a personal reminder. The card could also be placed in their writing folders or on a bulletin board. Remind the entire class to use the spelling strategy by merely pointing to the card.

Strategy 3-11: Trace, Cover, and Write for Study

"trace, cover, write it"

Observed Behavior

Charlie has a very hard time remembering new things, whether it is spelling words or vocabulary. He is very conscientious about studying for tests. He takes home lists which he uses as drills with help from his mother. His mother even makes flashcards for each thing he needs to learn. Yet he still barely passes his tests.

Charlie is not unlike many students who have great difficulty learning new spelling or vocabulary words. Although he appropriately uses written lists and flashcards to visually review information and does oral drills to review new information, he only retains about 70 percent of what he has studied. Charlie may be the kind of student who would be better able to put new information into his brain by placing it in many areas of memory simultaneously. Simply stated, this means we need to "bombard his senses." Thus, we must purposely put the new information into his visual memory, auditory memory, and motor memory at the same time. This style of instruction is labeled *multimodality input*. Placing information in many areas of the brain can help a student by spreading the ideas throughout the brain. With many connections throughout the brain, a student has more places from which ideas can be found. However, because many students can be overwhelmed with this approach, we must be very careful that we don't confuse them. This approach should only be used in very systematic, step-by-step instruction. "Trace, cover, write" is such a system. How do we teach it to Charlie?

Strategies and Tools to Improve the Student's Performance

1. Create an easy-to-follow form. Charlie can use this form to practice the words that he personally feels are challenging. A simplified form can be created on a vertically folded three-section piece of paper, with the center section containing his words/vocabulary list. Given a list to look at, Charlie can see, say, and spell the items for visual and auditory input. The two side sections are folded toward the center to cover the list while Charlie is tracing and writing for motor memory input.

Finally, he can check the words by comparing them to his original list. Remember, every time we encounter the word, we recall it more easily.

Multimodality instruction is especially helpful with <u>spelling words</u>. To improve Charlie's memory for spelling words, he must follow these steps.

First, he must see, say, and spell each word aloud. This activates his visual and auditory memories for the words.

Second, he traces each new word, which activates motor memory through handwriting.

Third, he rewrites each word from memory, which forces him to immediately recall the word as best he can.

Finally, he has an opportunity to check his accuracy. He can see the words again by opening the folded section. If he has made an error, he can change it by cross-checking with the original. The sample that follows should clarify the procedure for using multimodalities for spelling. It shows Charlie's spelling list for "trace, cover, and write."

Notice that Charlie's words in the sample are written very neatly with a thick line pen. The printing is purposely dark, so when the side section is folded over on top of the list, the words will bleed through enough for Charlie to see them. With words slightly visible, Charlie will be able to see them enough to trace them. Let Charlie dictate the words so an adult can be responsible for neat, dark writing.

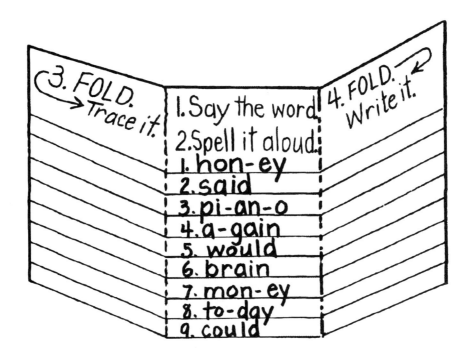

2. Use this recipe to instruct students about trace, cover, and write with spelling.

- Explain to students that they are going to learn a new way to study. They are going to put their new words into their brain by seeing, talking, spelling, tracing, writing, and checking, so the words are easier to remember.

- Show the form with words written down the middle section of the three-fold paper.

  ▶ *Alternative:* Ask the student to choose the words that need practice. Write them in syllables for the student in the middle section with a thick line pen. Number the list.

- Explain to students that they will do the first word along <u>with you</u> for all the steps.

  ▶ **Say:** "Look at the first word and read it aloud. Spell the word aloud. If the word has syllables, pause between syllables."

  ▶ **Say:** "*Fold* over the left-side section to cover the word. Look carefully to see the word peeking through the paper and trace it."

  ▶ **Say:** "*Fold* the right-side section to cover up the traced word. Try to remember and write the word."

  ▶ **Say:** "*Open the paper's folds* to check to see if the word is right. Fix the word if necessary."

- Tell students to try the next word alone. Remind them: First, read it and spell it aloud. Second, fold and trace it. Third, fold and write it without peeking. Last, check it and fix any errors.

- Interrupt when it appears the one word has been completed on the form. Ask if there are any questions. Answer any questions.

- Tell students to finish the task.

- Observe the students as they finish the task to note any frustration. At a later time review the strategy to ensure they understand its purpose.

3. Create a form for vocabulary study. This multimodality learning strategy can also be modified for *vocabulary words*. The task includes the same steps for: (1) reading/spelling aloud, (2) tracing, and (3) writing to put the new words into the parts of the brain that store visual ideas, auditory ideas, and motor ideas. However, we need to add a section for reviewing the definitions of new vocabulary words. The vocabulary list can be selected by the instructor or by the student. Remember, it is best to have an adult write the words for the students to make sure the writing is clear and dark enough to be seen through the folded paper for the tracing step in the procedure. The words should be numbered to increase the students' ability to keep track of the items while they are working through the entire task. The words should be written in syllables to encourage good spelling skills.

The recipe remains essentially the same as that given previously for spelling, with the exception of the definition section of the task. The vocabulary words are written in the middle section, skipping one space between items. This allows two lines of space for writing a definition directly across from the vocabulary word on the right-side section. After the words are written in the middle section of the folded paper, return the form to the student for writing in the definitions.

Here is a sample showing Charlie's vocabulary list for "trace, cover, and write."

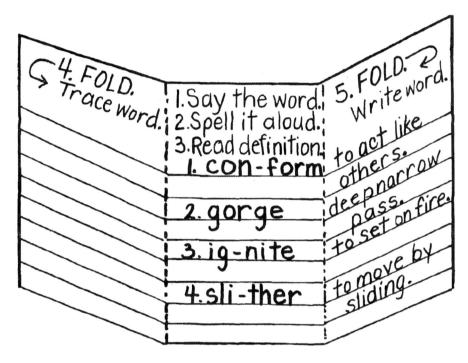

4. Use this recipe to instruct students about trace, cover, and write with vocabulary. (*Note:* The added steps as compared with spelling are in **bold**.)

- Explain to the students that they are going to learn a new way to study. They are going to put their new words into their brain by seeing, talking, spelling, tracing, writing, and checking, so that the words are easier to remember.

- Show the form with words written down the middle section of the three-fold paper.
  - ▶ *Alternative:* Ask the student to choose the words that need practice. Write them in syllables for the students in the middle section with a thick line pen. Number the list.
  - ▶ **Skip a line between each item to allow space for the definition.**

- Explain to students that they will do the first word along <u>with you</u> for all the steps.
  - ▶ **Say:** "Look at the first word and read it aloud. Spell the word aloud. If the word has syllables, pause between syllables."

▶ **Say: "Read the definition aloud for the new vocabulary word."**

▶ **Say:** *"Fold* the left-side section to cover the word. Look carefully to see the word peeking through the paper and trace it."

▶ **Say:** *"Fold* the right-side section to cover the traced word. Try to remember and write the word."

▶ **Say:** *"Open the paper's folds* to check to see if the word is right. Fix the word if necessary."

▶ **Say: "Try to remember the new word meaning without peeking. Check to see if you got it right."**

● Tell them to try the next word alone. Remind them: First, read it and spell it aloud. Second, fold and trace it. Third, fold and write it without peeking. Fourth, check it and fix any errors. **Last, try to remember the word meaning without peeking.**

● Interrupt when it appears the one word has been completed on the form. Ask if there are any questions. Answer any questions.

● Tell students to finish the task.

● Observe the students as they finish the task to note any frustration. At a later time, review the strategy to make sure they understood its purpose.

Worksheet

"Trace, Cover, and Write for Spelling"

This "Trace, Cover, and Write for Spelling" form is included for your convenience. Although this form is easily created on standard lined paper that is folded, students benefit from the headings that are listed on the form that would not be available on a simple folded paper.

3. FOLD.
Trace It.

1. Say the word.
2. Spell it aloud.

4. FOLD.
Write it.

1		
2		
3		
4		
5		
6		
7		
8		
9		
10		
11		
12		
13		
14		
15		
16		

Worksheet

"Trace, Cover, and Write for Vocabulary"

This form is included for the convenience of the instructor. Although this form is easily created on standard lined paper that is folded, students benefit from the headings that are listed on the form that would not be available on a simple folded paper.

5. FOLD. Write it.

1. Say the word.
2. Spell it aloud.
3. Read definition.

4. FOLD. Trace it.

1			
2			
3			
4			
5			
6			
7			
8			

Strategy 3-12: Association Strategy for "Stinker" Spelling Words   "associate it"

Observed Behavior

Ashley has trouble every time she tries to spell a word that does not exactly follow the rules of regular letter sounds. If a letter makes a specific sound, Ashley remembers only one way to spell it. Even when she looks at her written words, she does not consistently notice when words look wrong. After all, she has carefully "sounded out" each "noise" in the word, so she doesn't think of double-checking it visually.

Ashley—like many students—has mastered the sounds of letters for spelling phonetically regular words, but she rigidly applies the rules related to the sounds without considering the possibility of exceptions. Although she has a good use of skills for letter/sound relationships, ordering of letter sounds, and syllable concepts, she is very weak in her visual memory for words, which is manifested in her difficulty with recognizing that a word might look "funny." Her spelling problem is further complicated by the fact that a large number of words in the English language do not follow a strict set of rules. So, how do we teach Ashley to spell words that have irregular spellings?

Strategies and Tools to Improve the Student's Performance

As Ashley is unaware of the fact that words often contain irregular spellings, she must develop an awareness of this concept. This understanding will help her to more consciously re-check her words for possible "goofs." We can assist her with this by pointing out the letters that "don't play fair" within specific words. These letters are called "stinkers" because they do not follow the rules. Initially, we may have to tell her the exact error letter so she can mark it and practice it. However, this is probably not enough because she may not remember the next time she tries to spell a word that contains it. Instead, we need to go one step further and teach her to think about the specific "stinker" letter in the word and compare it to a similar word she does know how to spell. The process of linking a known word to a more difficult one creates an association between two ideas; thus, she will be better able to remember the difficult word later.

To start, instructors need to identify the letters within words that are irregular. The majority of spelling errors fall into one of six categories:

1. Silent letters (extra letters without sounds); example: *gost* vs. *ghost*

2. Consonants with varied sounds; example: *jiraffe* vs. *giraffe*

3. Double consonants (sh, ch, th, wh, ck, ng); example: *pikle* vs. *pickle*

4. Vowel letters in single-syllable words; example: *grate* vs. *great*

5. Vowel letters in multisyllable words; example: *toolip* vs. *tulip*

6. Irregular syllable patterns; example: *-tion* vs. *-sion*

Given these six examples as a general guideline for spelling error analysis, we will be better able to identify "stinker" letters within words for Ashley. It will be helpful to tell Ashley which category her letter errors fall into because this may help her begin noticing patterns in her errors and thus identify some of the error letters on her own. We must keep in mind, however, that this is a *general* guideline; our language is full of exceptions that may not fall into any of the above listed categories. This is further complicated by the fact that so many of our words come from other languages that have spelling rules that differ from our own.

Once the "stinker" letter or letters in a word are identified and marked in the spelling word, students will be ready to learn ways to remember the correct spelling for the difficult part of the word.

First, they must look carefully at the difficult part to see if that part looks like another word they already know. For example, given a choice of *here* or *hear*, which one means "using your ears"? The difficult part of the word is the vowel spelling. The student could look carefully and see "ear" in "hear."

Second, students need to associate the known word, "ear," to the more challenging spelling word, "hear." When we think of ways to remember one thing by comparing it to something else, we are making an association, or link, between ideas. No matter how we come up with the association, we must "hook" the idea to the meaning of the spelling word that is difficult for the student.

Third, students must be sure to put the two comparative ideas together in their visual imagination, either in a sentence or in an illustration. So, the students could create a sentence that contains both "ear" and "hear," such as "I can hear with my ears," to better remember. However, research has shown that the strongest tool for memory is visualization. So, when students can imagine how their association actually looks, they will recall it better. Students can use either mental visualization or drawing to create an illustration for the association.

Finally, students must learn to select their most efficient style for creating the association. For example, encourage the verbal learner to pause and imagine the sentence that is written. For the visual learner, encourage the use of drawing an illustration to convey the message of the sentence.

There are three general strategies that can assist students in recognizing known words within difficult parts of words by helping them to create associations for spelling:

1. Find a <u>small</u> word within the word.

2. Find a <u>rhyming</u> word within the word.

3. Find a <u>silly or clever</u> word within the word.

Students will need instruction in using these strategies for both one-syllable and multisyllable words.

1. Use three general strategies and dialogues for creating associations for spelling errors. The first spelling association strategy is to find a <u>small word</u> inside the difficult word that contains the correct spelling needed in the word.

- *An example of a hidden word in a single-syllable word is "paint" misspelled as "pant."* The letter that is incorrect is a missing "i." The correct spelling of "paint" has a silent "i" following the vowel "a." A hidden word that contains the missing "i" could be "pain." But how could "pain" have anything to do with "paint"?

  Remember, to form an effective association, students must connect two ideas so they are hooked together in memory. To connect "pain" and "paint," they could imagine a person "painting" with a "pain" in their back. **Say:** "Can you imagine a pain in the back as you paint? Could you draw a person painting with a pain in his or her back? Could you write a sentence with both words?" "Sure you could—'Peter got a pain in his back from painting the fence.'"

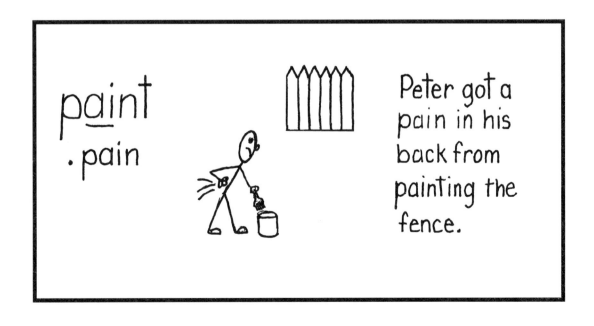

- *An example of a hidden word in a multisyllable word is "education" misspelled as "edukation."* The letter that is incorrect is "k." The correct spelling of "education" has a "c" instead of a "k." A hidden word that contains the "c" could be "cat." But how could a "cat" have anything to do with "education"?

  Remember, the students must be able to hook the two ideas together. They could imagine a "cat" getting an "education." **Say:** "Could you draw a cat in school? Could you write a sentence with both words? Sure you could—'The cat is sitting at school getting its education.'"

The second spelling association strategy is to use <u>rhyming words</u> for the difficult part of the word that contains the correct spelling needed in the word.

- *An example of a rhyme in a single-syllable word is "pail" misspelled as "pale."* The letter that is incorrect is the vowel "e." The correct spelling of "pail" has a silent vowel letter "i" following the "a." A rhyming word that contains the "i" could be "sail" with "pail"—and they look almost the same. But how could a "pail" have anything to do with a "sail"?

  Remember, students must hook the two ideas together. They could imagine a "pail" on a "sail" boat. **Say:** "Could you draw a pail on a sailboat? Could you write a sentence with both words? Sure you could—'The man took a pail on the sailboat in case he needed to bail out water.'" (This sentence uses three rhyming words!)

• *An example of a rhyme in a multisyllable word is "museum" misspelled as "muzeum."* The letter that is incorrect is the letter "z." The correct spelling of "museum" has an "s" instead of a "z." A rhyming word that contains the "s" could be "see." We could use the "see" to make the rhyme "You can see 'um in a museum." We would hear "see 'um" and remember that we SEE things in a muSEum. **Say:** "Could you draw a person seeing pictures in a museum? Could you write a sentence with both words? Sure you could—'Mom wanted to see the paintings, so we went to see 'um at the museum.'"

The third spelling association strategy is to use a <u>nonsense idea</u> for the difficult part of the word that contains the correct spelling needed in the word.

• *An example of a nonsense idea in a single syllable word is "break" misspelled as "brake."* The letter that is incorrect is the silent vowel "e." The correct spelling "break" has a vowel "e" preceding the vowel "a." If you take out the "r" letter, you can see the word "beak." But how could a "beak" have anything to do with "break"? The nonsense idea of a "beak" that "breaks" could be visualized as an imaginary bird with a beak that breaks. Silly, yes, but because it is silly, the students may remember it. **Say:** "Picture in your mind a bird with a broken beak. Could you draw it? Could you write a sentence with the words 'beak' and 'break'? Sure you could—'Don't feed nails to the bird; it might break his beak.'"

2. Use this recipe to instruct students about creating associations for spelling errors. This procedure is easily completed with individual students. For group instruction, you may want to determine which of the week's spelling words have "stinkers" and create a general class list. Don't waste time on words that are already known.

- Tell the students they are going to learn a new way to remember "stinker" letters in spelling words that are hard to remember. They will find tricks in words, and then draw their ideas and write a sentence for the ideas.

- Give the students a vertically folded paper with two sections.
    - ▶ See the sample task and worksheets at the end of this strategy section.
    - ▶ Tell students to carefully <u>print</u> (not cursive) the correct spelling of their error words in the left-hand section of the folded paper.
    - ▶ Tell them to underline the hard-to-remember letters (or trace them with a color) in the word where they made an error in their practice test.

- Ask, "Does the 'stinker' letter part of the word look like a <u>little word</u> you know?"
    - ▶ Wait for "thinking" time. Acknowledge any attempt. Give clues.
    - ▶ "Write the little word(s) you think of under the spelling word on your paper."

- Ask, "Could the 'stinker' letter part of the word be in a <u>rhyme word</u> you know?"
    - ▶ Wait. Acknowledge. Encourage. Give clues.
    - ▶ "Write the rhyme word(s) you think of under the spelling word on your paper."

- Ask, "Could the 'stinker' letter part of the word be part of a <u>crazy or silly idea</u>?"
    - ▶ "Could the silly word have something to do with the whole spelling word?"
    - ▶ Wait. Acknowledge. Encourage. Give clues.
    - ▶ "Write the crazy or silly word ideas under the spelling word on your paper."

- Now, <u>the most important part</u> is to decide which "stinker" idea word goes best with the meaning of the spelling word.

    ▶ Students may need assistance to decide how the "stinker" idea word fits together with the whole spelling word meaning to create a drawing or a sentence. Illustrated samples may be needed.

    ▶ "Mark the 'stinker' idea word you like the best."

- Ask, "Can you draw an illustration for the 'stinker' idea word and the whole spelling word?"

    ▶ "Draw it on the right-side section of the folded paper."

- Ask, "Can you make a sentence with the 'stinker' idea word and the whole spelling word?"

    ▶ "Write the sentence under the drawing."

- Repeat the above procedure for as many "stinker" words as you think are needed before asking the students to attempt it on their own (with adult supervision).

3. Use this idea for building home–school communication about spelling-error strategy. As the skill is learned, students could be asked to take home their pretest and complete the spelling association worksheet with a parent. The pretest could be accompanied by copies of:

1. the six general categories of spelling errors

2. three general association strategies with dialogue samples

3. the recipe, in case the parents might want to assist their child with the skill

Following is a <u>completed sample</u> showing Ashley's "stinker" spelling associations. Please note that Ashley was encouraged to draw visual configuration boxes around her "stinker" word. This was purposely done to improve her ability to notice the whole word shape and improve her visual memory for whole words.

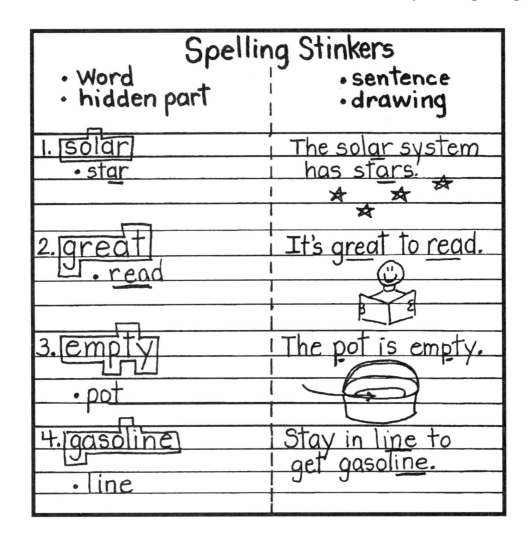

4. Use CUE CARDS to remind students to make associations for difficult spelling words. CUE CARDS such as the one that follows can be placed on their desks or in their spelling books as a visual reminder.

Worksheet

Creating Spelling Associations

This form for creating spelling associations is included for your convenience. Although this form is easily created on standard lined paper that is folded, students benefit from the headings that are listed on the form that would not be available on a simple folded paper.

Spelling Associations

-Write word.   -Write sentence.

-Write hidden words.   -Draw picture.

◉➤ Strategy 3-13: Association Strategy for New Vocabulary   "associate it"

Observed Behavior

Sidney can read with an understanding of the main ideas, but he cannot remember the new vocabulary. When asked to explain or write vocabulary meanings, he can quote the exact words from the book that he has memorized; however, he is unable to use his own words to tell what the word means. When tests use paraphrased definitions or meanings in varied contexts, he becomes confused and misses items because he has not truly understood them.

Many students have Sidney's problem. They study by memorizing information using often-repeated drills. Sidney reports that he has read the information, has written notes, and has orally practiced the new terms over and over again to try to remember them. Sidney is studying in a way that gives him a short-term memory of the information. All of his newly memorized information will probably fall out of his memory right after he takes the test for which he has specifically studied. This is unfortunate for all students because cumulative vocabulary knowledge will usually be retested in final exams, on high school graduation exams, and on SATs for college entrance. So, how do we teach Sidney to study and learn new vocabulary in a more effective way, so he will always remember it?

Strategies and Tools to Improve the Student's Performance

To learn difficult new vocabulary, Sidney must directly relate the new vocabulary to examples or situations that he has experienced. In other words, Sidney must learn a way to "hook" his old knowledge to the new vocabulary to get it permanently into his memory bank. In this way, he can transfer his short-term memory of the word into his long-term memory. Once it is in his long-term memory, he will be able to recall it. We can help him to put it there by finding key words or word parts that are hidden within the new vocabulary word. The logical step-by-step sequence for teaching the skill of vocabulary association is similar to the "stinker" spelling strategy.

Vocabulary association, though similar to spelling association, also must include a step that provides instruction on how to select hidden words, or key words, from inside the vocabulary word. Key words must be meaningful. They should be words that can be easily imagined or pictured in the students' minds. Key words that are names for specific people, objects, actions, or attributes are good sources for creating associations. Tiny words (*he, she, it, and, the*) and prepositions or position words (*in, on, up, down*) are often best ignored because they are difficult to imagine or draw.

The location of a key word can also be a factor. Certain parts of words provide more information about a word's meaning. It is helpful to point out to the students that it is often best to focus on the front area of a new word for identifying key words, as words are often filed or "clustered" into memory banks by their initial letters or sounds, similar to the dictionary. So, it would make sense to check the beginning of a new vocabulary term for possible key words. When students are able to recall the first syllable of a word, it more rapidly "triggers" the recall of the whole word.

When a root word or meaning clue sits in the middle of a word, the middle area of a word becomes the area of focus for finding a key word, because words are also filed or clustered in memory based on their meanings. Large multisyllable words often contain prefixes that precede <u>meaning-root words</u>, so to focus on the very beginning of the word, or the prefix, might not be the best choice. Once students locate their key words, they can combine them with the meaning of the new word and the new word itself to create a sentence that can be imagined and illustrated.

<u>The procedure for creating a vocabulary association involves five basic steps.</u>

First, the students must be given the word as well as an understandable definition. A discussion of the new meaning is beneficial, because it may trigger the students' memory of times they have heard or seen the word. After a discussion, the new word with its meaning should be written to stimulate visual and motor memory.

Second, the students should be asked to locate hidden words or partial words within the new vocabulary. The hidden words can be whole words, partial words, visually similar words, or rhyme words. Initially, the students should write any hidden word they find. With time and practice, they will begin to notice that the most effective words are those that represent real objects or actions that can be imagined or visualized easily.

Third, the students should examine all the hidden words they have found and determine which ones could have a connection to the new vocabulary word's meaning. It is best to select no more than one or two key words that "hook" to the new word's meaning.

Fourth, the students will be asked to create a sentence made up of the key word plus the new word plus the meaning. The sentence must be such that it can be pictured in the students' imagination. The ability to imagine or visualize the entire sentence is another means of putting new ideas in the brain. For study purposes, the students should underline the new word and the key words in their sentence.

Finally, the students illustrate the action of their written sentence. Drawing activates the visual memory area of the brain. As this skill is mastered, instructors will notice that students tend to select only one choice to express their key word connections for new words. They will choose to either write a sentence or create an illustration, whichever one fits with their personal style of remembering.

1. **Use this recipe to instruct students about associations for vocabulary.**
   - Explain that they are going to learn a new way to remember vocabulary.
   - Give students lined paper folded vertically in half.
     - ▶ Label the left side "vocabulary word/key words."
     - ▶ Label the right side "definition/associations."
     - ▶ A sample worksheet is included in this strategy section.
   - Ask the students to write the new vocabulary word in the left section.
   - Ask the students to copy your definition in the right section.
   - Discuss the meaning and how the word can be used.
     - ▶ Provide sentence examples that include the word.
     - ▶ Ask students to share their ideas.
   - Explain that they need to look for meaningful small words hidden within the larger vocabulary word.
     - ▶ Explain that the small words are called "key words" because they each have a meaning.
     - ▶ Tell them to <u>not</u> bother with tiny words or words that cannot be imagined in their minds.
   - Tell them to look carefully in the front of the word or at the main root words for ideas first.
     - ▶ Explain that if they can remember how a word starts, they usually remember the whole word.
     - ▶ Explain root words as compared to prefixes and suffixes if needed.
   - Ask, "Can you see any <u>hidden words</u> that can be imagined as real things or actions?"
     - ▶ "Write them under the vocabulary word on your paper."
   - Ask, "Can you think of any <u>words that begin with the same letters</u> as the vocabulary word?"
     - ▶ "Write them under the vocabulary word."
   - Ask, "Can you see any <u>rhyme words</u> for parts of the vocabulary word?"
     - ▶ "Write them under the vocabulary word."
   - Tell students to pick one or two of their hidden words that could have a connection to the vocabulary word's meaning. Think about how they could go together.
   - Tell students to write a sentence that shows how they go together.
     - ▶ "Write the sentence under the definition on the right side of your paper."
     - ▶ "Underline the key words and the new vocabulary word."

- Tell students to make a drawing to illustrate the things and the actions in their sentence.
    - ▶ "Put your drawing on the right side of the paper under your sentence."

Here is an example describing Sidney's completed vocabulary association.

- Sidney participated in the association 5-step sequence for the word "inundated."
- *First*, Sidney wrote the word and copied the definition the teacher suggested.
    - ▶ Inundated = being overwhelmed by something.
- *Second*, Sidney wrote key words found in "inundated" under the vocabulary word.
    - ▶ in
    - ▶ under
    - ▶ nun, tun, bun
    - ▶ date, dated
- *Third*, Sidney was asked, "Can any of your words be connected to being overwhelmed with? Are there any words that could describe a person or a thing that could overwhelm us?"
- *Fourth*, Sidney selected "dates." He could imagine being overwhelmed by dates.
- *Fifth*, Sidney wrote, "After winning the tennis tournament, Tim was inundated with dates."

Here is Sidney's drawing of his vocabulary association sentence, "After winning the tennis tournament, Tim was inundated with dates."

Here is Susie's drawing of her vocabulary association sentence. Sidney's friend Susie selected "nuns" as her key word. She could imagine being overwhelmed by nuns. Susie wrote, "I was inundated by nuns when I went to a church retreat."

inundated
•nuns

Note: This example purposely demonstrates two students' individual choices for the key word that they felt could be connected to the meaning of the word "inundated." In this example, the students found the same key words. Yet, because they have different experiences, they chose different words to create their associations. Both Sidney and Susie will remember their associations and the vocabulary word because they are personally meaningful. All students must be encouraged whenever possible to develop their own meaningful associations.

2. Use CUE CARDS to remind students to create "associations for difficult new vocabulary." The CUE CARDS can be placed on students' desks or in their spelling book as a visual reminder. *Note:* The illustration on the CUE CARD on page 218 depicts the creation of an association for <u>two</u> easily confused terms. The trick to keeping them straight is to create an association for *one* of the terms. The illustration created an association for "latitude" which contained the following key words: slat, latter, attitude, altitude, tude, rude. The student in the illustration chose "slat" meaning steps and "latter" because it rhymed with ladder. The illustration depicts a "ladder" . . . sounds like "latter." The student's sentence was, "I draw latitude lines from east to west like 'slat' steps on a 'latter.'" The student could then remember that the latitude lines, or "slat" steps, must be drawn horizontally from east to west.

Worksheet

Creating Vocabulary Associations

This form for creating vocabulary associations is included for your convenience. Although this form is easily created on standard lined paper that is folded, students benefit from the headings that are listed on the form that would not be available on a simple folded paper.

Note: It may be helpful to look at the illustration in the "draw it" strategy on page 146, which shows a completed student worksheet.

Vocabulary Associations

-Write vocabulary word.
-Write hidden key word ideas.

-Write definition.
-Write association sentence and/or draw illustration.

1.	

Section Four

Organization-Enhancing Strategies

· · · · · · · · · · · · · · · · · · ·

What's Included in Being Able to Organize Learning?

When learning becomes complex, that is, dependent upon many skills or many steps in a specific sequence, the quality of a student's performance can decrease unless a system is in place that keeps track of the parts. Although many students have the ability to organize and maintain the parts, some students get lost as they shift back and forth between them. Struggling students who are not confident about their basic skills are particularly at risk for these complex tasks.

What is a complex task? It is a task that is built on the mastery of many skills. Weakness in any of the basic skills required for the complex task will reduce the quality of a student's performance. Success with complex tasks is also built on a student's ability to shift back and forth between skills to produce an end product. Successful back-and-forth shifting requires that the students be able to remember where they were when they first shifted, so they can return to the correct place and know how to proceed. This ability to remember where we are in a process while we are doing something else is called "working" memory.

An example of a complex task in the content area of *math* is the process of long division. For long division, the students must have mastered the basic facts and the basic operations for subtraction, multiplication, and division. Without these skills stored solidly in memory, students will be unable to perform long division. Students who are unable to recall basic facts may need an interim organizational strategy—such as a multiplication grid—with which they can locate specific facts without being forced to add up sets of numbers to reach a multiplication-fact answer. If students are to be able to accurately complete long division problems, they must also know the correct sequence for using the operations. Even if students know how to do long division, they must be able to find and return to their place in the process, in case they are interrupted midway through a problem. Interruptions occur naturally in complex processes wherein the student must shift to think or perform a "side operation" and then bring the result of the side operation back to the task. In long division, for example, students may need to figure out how many times a divisor goes into a number, so they must move off to one side of the problem, multiply the divisor by a couple of numbers to determine which one fits, and then return to the original division problem to insert the correct number. In order to proceed, students must quickly and efficiently determine where the number fits into the division problem. To do this, they may need a visible recipe card for the steps on which they can keep track of each step as it is completed.

One example of a complex task in the content area of *written language* is the process of writing a paragraph. To successfully write paragraphs, students must have mastered basic skills for sentence structure, spelling, grammar, punctuation, ordering of ideas, and editing. Students who are unable to remember the essential parts of a sentence may need an interim organizational strategy—such as a sentence diagram chart—against which they can visually check the sentences' completeness. Or they might need to activate a strategy of "orally" re-reading each sentence so they can hear its grammatical accuracy before they proceed to the next sentence. Even when basic sentence structure skills are mastered, the students must be able to first organize their key ideas on the topic and then hold them in memory while they are putting the words together for the first sentence. On completion of the first sentence, they can then revisit their general ideas to determine which is the most logical idea about which to write the next sentence. Without the ability to return to general "planning" of the important ideas, students will be unable to logically organize their sentences in the paragraph. So, they may need a visual organizer on which to write their key ideas prior to beginning the sentence-writing step. In this way, they can more easily move back and forth between idea planning and sentence organization.

Struggling students can become very frustrated at this complex stage of learning that requires extensive memory skills. They often are particularly frustrated with the energy needed for holding ideas in their working memory while they do something else. These students will benefit from being provided with an organizational system with which they can keep track of the order for a complex task. It is essential to provide them with a visible and consistent organizational system to help them recall the appropriate sequence for completing a complex task.

However, not just any system will meet a specific student's needs. To be effective, it is important to match or adapt a system to the student's personal memory strength so that it will be easier to recall. An organizational system for a student with a visual learning style would then naturally be illustrated, graphically designed, and/or colored so the student could "see" it. An organizational system for a student with a sound/auditory learning style would best be practiced through speaking, reading, rhyme, or limericks so the student could "hear" it. A system for a student with a tactile-kinesthetic learning style would be touched, acted out with motions, or traced so the student could "feel" it. For example, a student can learn to read through the use of varied systems: phonetic (sound), word families or patterns that are repeated in words (vision), and mouth movements for sound (kinesthetic). Instructors must choose the system that, when practiced, best matches their students' memory strengths.

How Are the Organization Strategies Organized?

The strategies that follow this introduction include techniques that are similar in structure to the memory strategies. However, the strategies on organization must provide for one essential difference that is not part of students' memory strategy. Tools must be provided that enable students to hold one concept in their memory as they shift to another component of the task and then return to the initial concept. So, the organizational strategies that follow include specific recipes, illustrations, or worksheets that students can use to keep track of the steps that will enable them to move back and forth between parts of a complex task.

You will notice that this section does not include as many strategies as other sections. This is because their explanations would be very lengthy. Instead, specific strategies were chosen to demonstrate varied techniques for organizing instruction that could serve as models or guides for instructors. The selected strategies focus on:

1. Breaking down large concepts into smaller units. This is done by:
   - Mastering regular consonant letter sounds
   - Mastering irregular consonant letter sounds
   - Decoding words with vowel sound patterns
   - Performing complex multidigit multiplication
   - Performing complex long division
   - Organizing for paragraph writing

2. Utilizing materials or approaches that match students' personal learning styles or memory strengths. This is achieved by:
   - Using visual picture clues for auditory sounds of letters
   - Breaking words into smaller visual "chunks"
   - Using concrete materials to represent abstract math processes
   - Using visual model-problems to consult to check math accuracy
   - Following verbal scripts for calculating complex math operations
   - Using visual drawing for written language planning
   - Using visual organization tools for planning written tasks

By presenting the strategies in this general way, it is hoped instructors will be able to create their own personal organizational strategies that will target their struggling students.

You also will notice that, in contrast to earlier sections, this section provides more information on the particular kind of learner who would benefit most from each specific organizational strategy. The learning and memory styles of the individual student often dictate how you choose a successful organizational system for that student. The student behavior description, which precedes each organizational strategy, will be very important to the instructor, as it will shed light on the type of learner for whom the strategy would be the most effective.

To increase the instructor's ability to efficiently select strategies from this section, the strategies are clustered into three subject area categories: reading organization, math organization, and written-language organization. Most of the strategies include visual layout worksheets and pictorial examples for use in instruction that can be adapted for specific concept learning.

Strategy 4-1: Letter Sounds for the Alphabet Through Picture Tracing

"what's the picture?"

Observed Behavior

Willie is completing a matching task that requires him to look at a picture of an object and match it to a beginning letter sound. Although he is able to name the picture orally, he is unable to consistently identify the letter sound it begins with or draw a matching line between the picture and the correct letter on his paper. The only time he is successful is when he looks up at the illustrated alphabet picture chart at the front of the class. Even then he makes mistakes because he is not naming the pictures on the chart correctly.

Willie has not learned all the sounds that match the letter symbols. His teacher has provided instruction following a curriculum that focuses on phonetic concepts, or letter-sound mastery through listening. The ability to learn sounds through phonetics demands that Willie be able to hear and discriminate between differences in sounds and match them to a printed letter symbol. Although this skill is essential for learning to read, Willie is not mastering the skill through his hearing or auditory memory.

It is very important to notice that Willie depends on the illustrations on the alphabet chart to help him remember some of the sounds. He is instinctively using pictures to help with a "sound" skill. He knows that the pictures help, yet he is unable to remember the illustrations without looking up at the chart. How do we help Willie learn all the letter sounds in a more organized manner, using his visual memory strength? How do we select pictures for letter sounds that are meaningful to Willie? How do we ensure that he will remember the pictures and will not need to look up at a chart?

A brief look at history illustrates that this concept of using pictures for letter sounds is not new to the world of education. Educators have attempted to use illustrations as a medium for teaching letter sounds since the 1600s in England, with Comenius's *Orbis Sensualium Pictus*, believed to be one of the earliest children's books to include illustrations for the letters of the alphabet. During the early nineteeth century, as literacy grew, many books designed to teach the alphabet through pictures were published. These books often contained at least twenty-six pages, with illustrations for each alphabet letter; two examples are *The Picture Alphabet* by Oliver Spafford (1850) and *An Alphabet* by William Nicholson (1898).

In the early history of education, the primary focus of teaching reading skills was through the sensory mode of vision. Alphabet books were created based on categories of illustrations such as mythical creatures, nursery rhymes, toys, animals, fruits, flowers, and even comical actions. Over time, many of these letter pictures evolved into universally accepted illustrations for specific letter symbols. A few examples are the pictures for "a" being an apple, "c" being a cat, "d" being a dog, "q" being a queen, "s" being a snake, and "v" being a valentine. These have appeared in numerous alphabets.

Although visual alphabet systems continued to be developed throughout the centuries and into present time, the primary focus of instruction for most reading curriculums available today has shifted from visual to auditory mode for teaching letter-sound mastery. This is not to say that current alphabet curriculums do not include letter illustrations. However, because teachers' manuals tend to focus on phonetic, or sound, instruction, the illustrations are often not thoroughly explored with students.

Strategies and Tools to Improve the Student's Performance

So, how do we teach visual learners to use the illustrations so they will remember the picture names that match the individual letter sounds? For a student like Willie, who is struggling with recalling even some of the letter sounds, we must focus on his difficulty remembering the pictures on the classroom alphabet chart.

First, we must make sure that we select a visual alphabet that is meaningful to students. Should an alphabet contain a picture that is unknown, the students will need to participate in activities that include the picture item, so they can learn to recognize it and name it in order to "hear" the sound with which it begins. For example, one of the universally accepted pictures for the letter "i" is an igloo. Students will need to recognize the "igloo" picture and that the embedded "i" represents the escaping smoke from the igloo inhabitant's fire.

How do we help Willie remember the pictures for letter sounds without having to look up repeatedly at the alphabet chart? Even given a meaningful set of alphabet illustrations, the student might not be able to look at a letter symbol and recall the picture that matches the letter sound.

Second, we must find pictures that, when drawn around the letter symbol, match the actual shape of the letter. For example, the universally accepted "valentine" for the "v" letter symbol, which contains two slanted lines that meet in a point, can look very similar to the bottom half of a valentine. This is especially true if the students imagine, or visualize, the added top curves of the valentine and the lace-lines around the edge. In this way, Willie would not need to look up at the classroom alphabet to recall the "valentine" word for "v." Instead, the shape of the letter symbol alone would trigger his visual memory for the "valentine" sound clue.

How do we help Willie increase his ability to remember *all* the pictures that match *all* the letter symbols? To ensure his mastery of the pictures, we could add the use of an additional memory source—motor memory.

Third, activate the students' motor memory for the pictures by encouraging them to trace the pictures around the actual letter shapes so they can feel and see the movement of their hand as they draw. Willie would then have systematically placed the letter pictures in both his visual and motor memory banks. Most visually adept students also have skills in art, spatial concepts, and drawing, so the act of tracing and/or drawing may come naturally. However, we must take into consideration that fine motor control for drawing is often not fully developed until middle elementary school years. As a result, we need to provide models of drawings around letter shapes for the students to trace rather than ask them to draw on their own. The pictures must be very simple with minimal details, so they can be easily traced or drawn. For example, tracing the "snake" for the "s" shape would only require making an extra line parallel to the "s" shape and adding a snake's head and wiggling tongue. With simplified drawings such as these, visually adept students may even be able to draw the pictures on their own, but it should not be required.

Although each variable above is critical for developing an organized system for teaching the visual learner about the sounds of the letters, the instructor must understand <u>two additional critical concepts</u> prior to teaching the student.

First, the picture name is a word; as such, it contains many sounds, not just the initial letter sound.

Second, the picture word's first sound must be separated from the remainder of the word to be pronounced correctly. The instructor will need to teach visual students how to "freeze their mouth" immediately after they make the first sound as they are saying the whole word for the picture. The students must not attach the vowel sound to the initial consonant. This takes practice.

Instructors must keep in mind that they are teaching visual learners, so "telling" them how to separate the whole word into two parts will not make sense. Although most early elementary students have not yet learned to read whole words, instructors must show students how to visually break a word into the two parts. To do this, print the word as a whole and in parts so the students can see it. Only by seeing the separateness of the first letter can visual learners see that they must "produce" only the first part of the spoken word to know the first letter sound. This demonstration of "breaking" the word into parts also provides the students with an introduction to the concept that words have many letters.

1. Prior to introducing the concept of letter sounds, demonstrate the following facts.

> **Say:** "Our alphabet contains twenty-six letters. We have two sets of letters." (Show them to the students.) "One set is capital letters." (Have the students count them.) "The other set is called lowercase letters." (Have the students count them, then match the sets in two parallel vertical columns to show the pairs. *Optional:* Point to letters as students sing the "ABC Song.")
>
> **Say:** "Letters were invented so we could write words for reading." (*Optional:* Show other alphabets, for example, Egyptian hieroglyphics or Greek letters.)

> **Say:** "Words almost always contain more than one letter except for 'I' and 'a.'" (Explain and demonstrate that most reading words contain lowercase letters by writing out students' or their friends' names, so they can count the letters and see the differences in word lengths. Point out that names begin with capitals.)

For young learners, the visual illustrations for letter sounds are best introduced in the same order as the alphabet. Most children come to school with a beginning knowledge of the alphabet from years of home instruction, singing the "ABC Song," and/or watching educational television. Using the natural order of the alphabet for presenting letters initially, instruction will be built on what the student already knows. New learning is always easier when we build on top of a student's prior knowledge. So, for the emergent reader, the letter "a" is the perfect place to start. However, should the student know a majority of the letter sounds, select only the sounds that have not been learned yet.

2. Use the following recipe to instruct students about the pictograph for the letter "a." (Replace the **bold** print items when you introduce each new letter sound.)

- Explain the concept that remembering is often easier with pictures.

- Enlarge and show the selected letter with overlapping picture. Ask, "Can you see the letter **a** hiding in the picture?" Ask, "Can you see how the picture fits the letter exactly?" Ask, "Can you see the **apple** picture?"

- Give the students a copy of the letter with overlapping picture. Ask them:
  - ▶ *First*, finger-trace the **a** letter that is hiding.
  - ▶ *Next*, finger-trace the **apple** picture.

- Explain the picture's importance—that the name of the picture starts with the sound of the letter. Print out the whole word, saying, "This is the word **apple** for the picture. The first letter is **a**. It is the letter we are learning."

- Explain the need for only the first letter sound of the word. *Say:* "How can we take off the first letter so we hear only that part? I will show you. We are going to freeze our mouth for a short time on the first sound of the word."

- Print the word with the first letter **(a−pple)** separated from the rest of the word. *Say:* "Watch me as I freeze the word." Using an exaggerated motion, point as you freeze the word. Then instruct them to do it. Remember, do not include the next letter in the freeze part.

- Ask students to freeze the word as you slowly point at the parts. *Say:* "Right. The letter **a** in the picture word **apple** makes the freeze sound **a−pple**." Ask the students to repeat the sentence as you point to the letter/picture.

- Give the students a printed worksheet for letter **a** like the illustrated sample for "c" on page 228. Explain that they are going to use tracing, so they can remember better. Ask the students:
  - ▶ *First*, to trace the letter **a** with one color.
  - ▶ *Next*, to choose a new color and trace the **apple** picture.
  - ▶ *Last*, if they want, draw the picture around the letter on their own. (*Optional:* Place completed worksheet in a Letter Sound Book.)

- Once two letter-pictures are learned, give students a mixed set of picture words. Ask them to freeze/sort them by beginning letter sound. (Assist in task if needed.)

- Repeat this procedure for each letter. (*Optional:* After three or four letters, do a mixed task.)

Here is an initial set of pictures for the twenty-six letters of the alphabet (only regular consonants and short vowels). An enlarged set can be found at the end of this strategy.

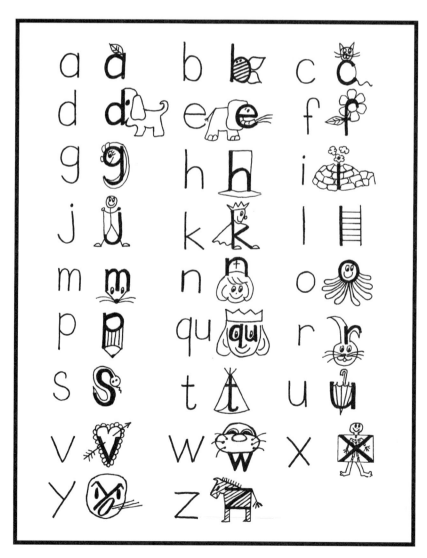

3. After students have learned one picture for each letter of the alphabet, review the visually *confusing pairs of letters***, placing the letters and pictures side-by-side to improve students' ability to distinguish the differences between the letters.** The visually confusing letter pairs are: **b** and **d**, **p** and **q**, **g** and **j**, **u** and **n**, **t** and **f**, and **v** and **w**.

- The **b** and **d** pair is confusing because they both contain a stick and a circle, but in different order.

- The **p** and **q** pair is confusing for the same reason.

- The **g** and **j** pair is confusing because they both contain a curve at the bottom.

- The **u** and **n** pair is confusing because although they both contain an open curve, one is open at the top and the other is open at the bottom.

- The **f** and **t** pair is confusing because although they both have a hook or curve, one is at the top and one is at the bottom.

- The **v** and **w** pair is confusing because they both have slanted line points.

For students who encounter difficulty with letter reversals, please refer to the strategies included in Section Two, Attention-Enhancing Strategies.

4. Use the following sample task for comparing visually confusing letter pairs. Students should be guided in the analysis of letter parts. They may need reminders to use the directional left-to-right arrow to help notice which stroke comes first in each letter. Illustrations for all letters can be found at the end of the strategy section and used to create additional worksheets.

Two letters look the same

Trace the letter part that comes first.

After students have mastered a majority of the basic letter sounds and understand that each letter has its very own sound, they should be exposed to the concept that *some letters may have more than one sound*. The consonant letters that have more than one sound are: **c**, **g**, **qu**, **x**, **y**. These letters actually "take" sounds from other letters.

5. Use this description of consonant letters that don't follow the one-sound rule.

- The letter **c** actually has no sound of its own because it takes the sounds of other letters. It takes the sounds of **k** and **s**. Most of the time, **c** takes the **k** sound. Look in the dictionary and find the **k** words; you will see how very few words start with **k**. That's because **c** took most of them.

- The letter **g** can have a hard, back-of-the-throat sound that is made with the lip open. That's the regular sound of **g**. Sometimes the **g** can have a soft, front-of-the-mouth sound that is made with the lips slightly puckered. That sound really belongs to **j**, but the letter **g** takes the **j** sound for words like: *giraffe, giant, gym,* and *ginger*.

- The letter **q** sounds like "queen," yet students should be told that the first sound in *queen* is actually spelled as **qu**. The "qu" takes sounds from two letters and puts them together for the sound **k** + **w**.

- *(Optional:)* The letter **x** can sound like "x-ray" and "xylophone." The word "x-ray" begins with **x**, but if you say the word slowly, you will feel the sound of **k** plus **s** coming before the **r** that comes next in "x-ray." So **x** actually takes two sounds and puts them together. This **x** sound does not often come at the front of words, but there are lots of words with **x** in the middle and end of words. The word "xylophone" begins with **x**, but it takes the sound of **z**. Very few words begin with the **z** sound for **x**.

- *(Optional:)* The letter **y** sounds like "yell" at the beginning of words, but it acts like a vowel inside words, so it has to take vowel sounds. The letter **y** can steal vowel sounds like: short **i** in *cymbal* and *gym*, long **i** in *fly* and *cry*, and long **e** in *baby*.

Although this concept is complex, it is important that students understand that some letters have two different sounds. This is especially true for **c** and **g** because these letters appear frequently in words. Students must be prepared with the knowledge that they can shift a **c** and **g** sound in a puzzling word to a different sound and thus figure out more words on their own.

Introduce the "two sounds for a letter" concept with the letter **c**. Provide students with side-by-side pictures for the *two c sounds* for comparing the **c** as "cat" to the **c** as "cent."

6. Use this sample tracing task showing the two sound pictures for the letter "c." The layout of this task can be used as a guide for creating a **g** tracing task for students.

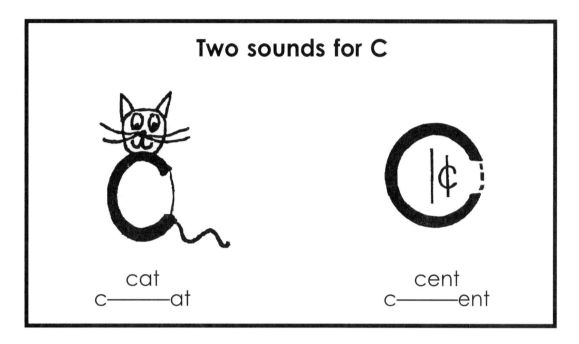

The recipe for comparing two sounds in the next strategy section can be used as a guide for introducing these letters. Complete the instruction steps for: (1) naming the pictures, (2) tracing the letters/pictures, (3) printing the words for pictures, (4) breaking the words, and (5) "freezing" the words to hear/feel the first sounds of the picture words.

Visual students are quick to notice that the words "cat" and "cent" begin with the same visible letter, yet the letter makes a different sound. Students should not have difficulty recognizing the sounds, because the **k** and **s** sounds had previously been learned. Students can quickly master this concept with the sorting of pictures for varied **c** words. The instructor should guide the task by saying each picture word with an exaggerated stress on the first sound. The student would then match the picture to the correct **c** sound. The sample task that follows can be adapted for other "two-sound" letters.

7. Use the following "Mr. C" sample task for sorting pictures/words with different sounds for the same consonant. This task should be used as a guide for creating worksheets for the other letters that have two sounds. For example, the "Mr. C" could be changed to "Mr. G" with new sorting pictures that begin with the letter **g**. The two sounds for letters **x** and **y** should be introduced by comparing the pictures and letter illustrations, so students would at least be aware of the fact that these letters can have more than one sound.

Cut out and glue the pictures in the right sound box.

Vowel letters also have more than one sound, but at the early stage of reading, students are not ready to learn all the sounds possible for vowels. They should be told that the letters A–E–I–O–U are special letters called vowels. They can have more than one sound, just like the **c**, **g**, **x**, and **y**.

A simple introduction to this vowel concept can be demonstrated with visual illustration of the vowel letter a, which the student has already learned as **a** sounds like "apple." The "a for apple" illustration can be compared to the "a for angel" illustration. The "a for angel" makes a different sound that students will later learn as a long vowel sound. The two pictures can be traced or drawn side-by-side on paper so they can see the difference in the pictures surrounding the same letter. Students can freeze the words and use a mirror to compare the sounds and the mouth movements. The pairs of pictures should be demonstrated for all five vowels, so students can see that ALL VOWELS have more than one sound.

8. Use this sample tracing task for learning the two sound pictures for the vowel letter "a." This should be used as a guide for creating worksheets for the other "two sounds for vowel letters." Illustrations for all the vowels are provided at the end of this strategy section.

This strategy and the next were purposely selected to demonstrate how critical it is to match the mode of instruction to the student's memory strength. Without instruction in using visual information plus the use of motor memory in copying pictures, Willie might have continued to struggle with learning the letter sounds. Over time, he might have learned a set of pictures for letter sounds on his own, but he would have lost valuable time and the opportunity to feel confident about his reading.

Worksheets

Ready-to-Use Pictures for Regular Letter Sounds

The letter pictures can be enlarged for making worksheets, classroom charts, and cards for sorting.

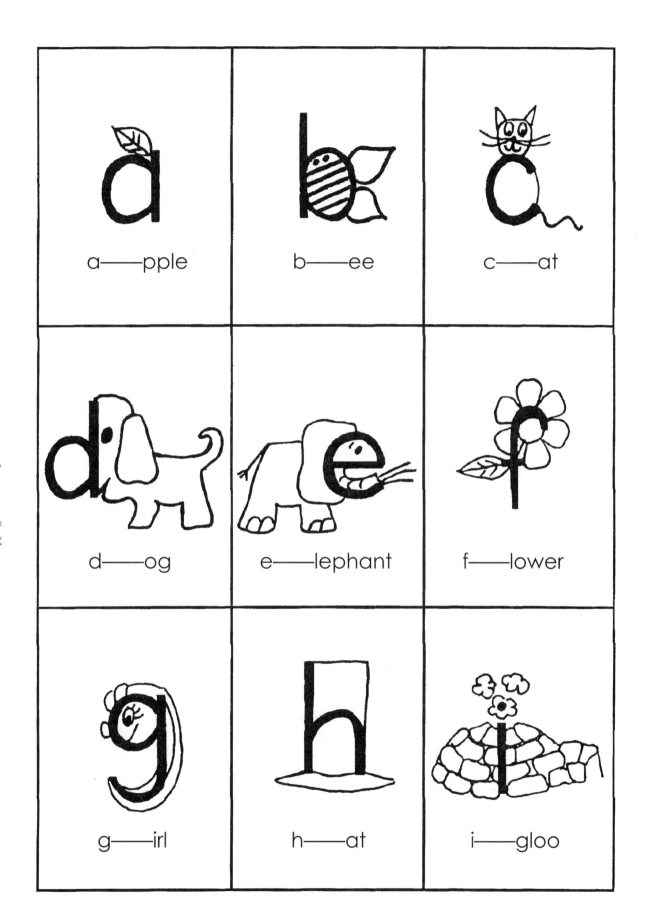

a——pple

b——ee

c——at

d——og

e——lephant

f——lower

g——irl

h——at

i——gloo

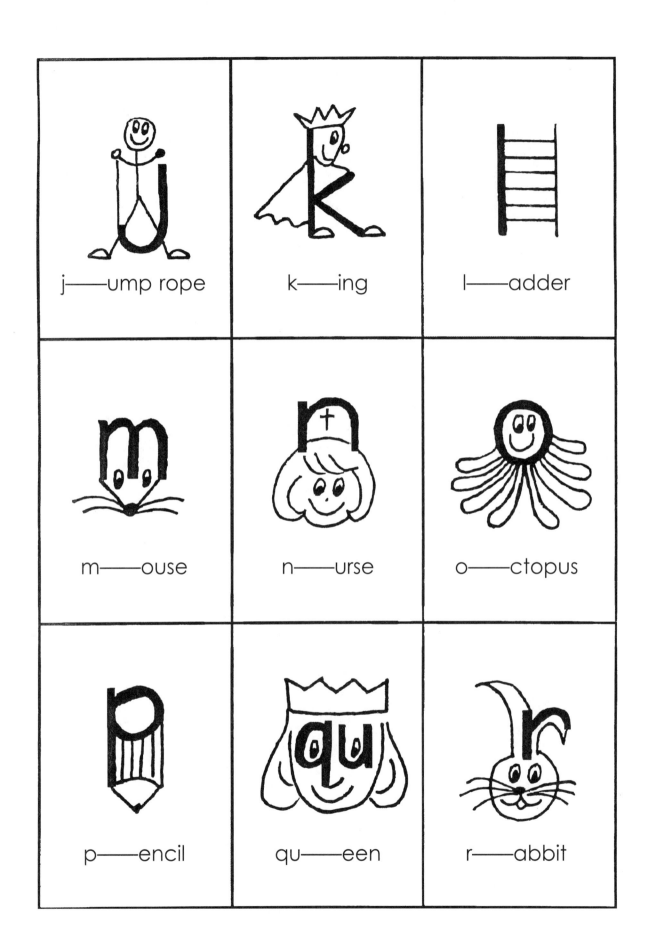

j—ump rope

k—ing

l—adder

m—ouse

n—urse

o—ctopus

p—encil

qu—een

r—abbit

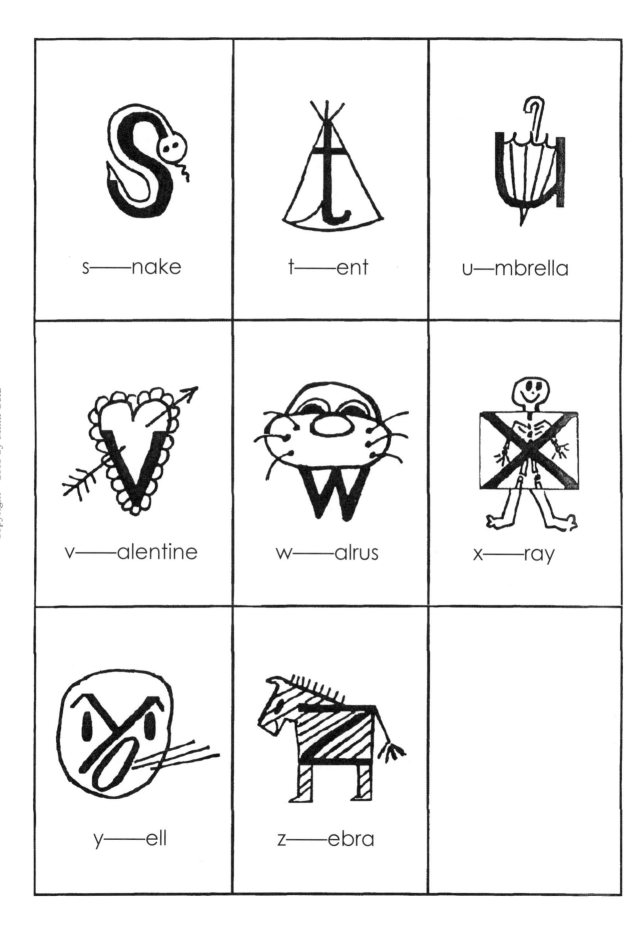

s—nake t—ent u—mbrella

v—alentine w—alrus x—ray

y—ell z—ebra

Worksheets

Ready-to-Use Pictures for Letters with Two Sounds

The letter pictures can be enlarged for making worksheets, classroom charts, and cards for sorting.

 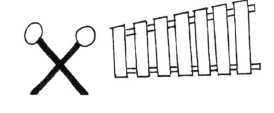

**Vowel Letters
Can Have
Two Sounds**

a——ngel

e——agle

i——ce cube

o——pen can

u——nicorn

c——ent

g——iraffe

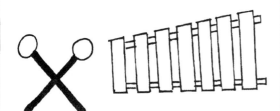

x——ylophone

cy——mbals
(letter y in the middle)

cry
(letter y at the end)

happy
(letter y at the end)

Strategy 4-2: Digraph Letter Sounds Through Picture Tracing "what's the picture?"

Observed Behavior

Mario has learned the regular consonant sounds for single letters with visual pictures. Yet he remains very confused when new words contain double letters that make only one sound. He sees the word thin *and can tell his teacher the letters in the word, but makes the "t" sound. Then he checks the "h," the "i," and "n," but makes separate sounds for each letter. He grimaces as he says the word with the four sounds, because he knows it sounds "funny." He looks at the alphabet chart to check. He knows by the teacher's face that he is wrong, but he does not know how to ask for help.*

Mario has incorrectly applied the rule of "Each letter makes one sound." He has not learned that some letters can sit next to each other in a word and make a different sound. He may not have seen real words that contain double-letter sounds. These letter pairs are called *consonant digraphs*. The letter pairs are: **ch**, **ph**, **sh**, **th**, **wh**, and **ng**. Knowing of Mario's past success with learning the regular consonant letter sounds through pictures, we can apply the same strategy to teach him about *digraph letters*.

Strategies and Tools to Improve the Student's Performance

Mario must understand that the digraph pairs break the "one sound" rule. He will need to see the pictures that match the letter pairs. He will also need to trace the pictures and the letters. Finally, he will need to learn how to freeze the digraph sounds in real words. If students are to master digraph sounds, they must be able to systematically compare the new digraph sound to the regular consonant sound.

Before beginning to teach about the digraphs, the instructor should understand how to use <u>two additional concepts</u> that are very effective with visual learners.

First, students can actually see and compare mouth movements used in their pronunciation of digraphs versus the single-letter consonant sounds, for example, **ch** compared to **c**. By watching their mouth in a hand-held mirror or by watching a "buddy" make the sounds with his or her mouth, the visual learner can easily analyze mouth movements to increase memory of the specific movements for each sound.

Here is a list of <u>mouth movements</u> showing digraph sounds compared with regular consonants. (For further information, see *Applied Phonetics* by Harold Edwards, published by Singular Pub. Group, 1992.)

- The **ch** sound jumps out of puckered lips as compared to the **c** which stays in the back of the throat.

- The **ph** sound makes the same sound as **f**, or air coming out across the bottom lip and the teeth, as compared to the **p** which comes out of both lips.

- The **sh** sound flows out of puckered lips like a teacher telling you to be "quiet," as compared to the **s** which comes out "hissing" between the visible front teeth.

- The **th** sound makes the tongue stick out a little bit, as compared to the **t** which keeps the tongue in the mouth and moving up and down.

- The **wh** and **w** sounds are harder to compare. Students may be able to see that both are made with lips together, but the **wh** *whi*spers quietly without sound in the voice box and looks like it is trying to blow out candles on a cake.

The *second* essential concept, easily recognized by visual learners, involves noticing that the first five digraphs <u>all contain an **h** letter</u>. Without viewing them in a group, Mario probably would not notice the repeated use of **h**. Humor can be used to explain the important "job" of the letter **h** in the digraphs. Students giggle when they are told that the **h** is really nasty, because he often yells at certain consonant letters in front of him. He tells them to "be quiet" and make a new sound because he's boss in digraphs. So, whenever Mario sees an "h" that is sitting behind the letter **c**, **p**, **s**, **t**, or **w**, he will know that **h** will be a "Grouchy Guy."

Based on the visual learner's ability to recall pictures for concepts, it may be helpful to show an illustration for the "Grouchy **h** Guy" as reaching over and tapping the first letter on the head. After the instruction for all digraphs is completed, Mario will benefit from seeing all the **h** digraphs in a column so he can see the repeated **h** pattern in one visual display.

1. Adapt the following "Grouchy <u>h</u> Guy" illustration for all "h" digraphs. Students could be asked to draw the "Grouchy **h** Guy" around the **h** on a worksheet that contains mixed pairs of digraphs and two-letter blends.

With the use of these two concepts—viewing mouth movements and noticing the **h** in digraphs—the instructor will be prepared for success with the students. The instructor will, of course, need the pictures that match each letter pair. (A sample worksheet with the pictures for **ch** versus **c** is included as a model for creating the

other digraph sound worksheets.) Finally, the instructor will need a suggested recipe, such as the one that follows later in this strategy, for teaching the digraphs to the students.

These are pictographs for the digraph letter sounds of **ch**, **ph**, **sh**, **th**, and **wh**.

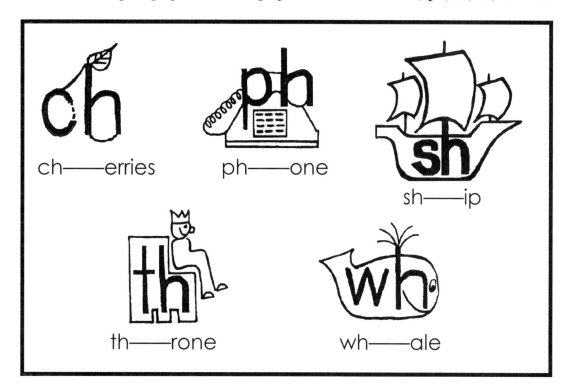

ch——erries   ph——one   sh——ip

th——rone   wh——ale

2. Use this sample tracing task to teach the sound of "ch" versus "c."

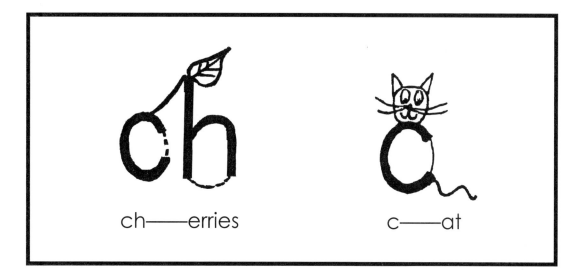

ch——erries   c——at

3. Use the following recipe to instruct students in how to compare a digraph with a regular consonant sound (ch versus c). (*Note:* Replace the **bold** phrases for each new digraph.)

- Give the students the sample task with both **ch** and **c** letter/pictures and the "freeze" printed words for each letter/picture. Ask what is different in the two. Ask them to trace the letters, the picture, and the word **cherries** for **ch**. Ask them to do the same with **c** for **cat**. Show/point how the words begin with the same letter, but they don't make the same sound. Tell them "h" changes the **c**.

- Print the words as wholes and then *reprint* them with the first sound separated from the rest of the word: **ch—erries**, **c—at**. Ask them if they can see the "h" in the "freeze part" of the cherries. Tell them how "h" changes the **c** because it is the boss in digraphs.

- Freeze each word to compare the sounds. Remember, do not include the next sound in the freeze part. Demonstrate how different the mouth looks when **ch** is sounded as compared to **c**. Use a mirror or choose a partner, so the student can watch someone's mouth movement. With **ch**, the sound jumps out of puckered lips as compared to the **c** which stays in the back of the throat.

- Give students a mixed set of pictures with both **ch** and **c** initial letter sounds and ask them to freeze/sort them by beginning letter sound. (*Optional:* Use a mirror.)

- Repeat this procedure for each digraph sound.

The letter pair **ng** is also a digraph because it contains two letters that make one sound. It looks different because it does not contain an **h** letter. The **ng** sound is also more difficult to recognize because it is always at the end of a word or a syllable. An example would be the word "ring." So, when you provide the students with an illustration, you must clearly explain that it can never be found at the front of a word. The illustration for the **ng** sound is "King Kong." The **n** and **g** letters become the long arms of the gorilla.

4. Use the following King Kong illustration to teach the digraph "ng."

It is critical for the visual learner to see words that contain the **ng** at the end. Examples of appropriate words could be *bang, ring,* and *gong.* However, it may be more meaningful for the visual learner, who may enjoy rhyme, to use sets of rhyming words to see the **ng** letters repeated in the rhyming words. Use the following sets of rhyming words that contain the same vowels: *bang-fang-hang, king-sing-wing, gong-song-long,* and *hung-rung-sung.* By using sets of rhyming words, the visual learner could see the repeated vowel patterns in real words.

An additional strategy for understanding the **ng** digraph is to use the mirror or a buddy. The student can say an **ng** word and see the tongue move to the back of the mouth. Words that contain the short vowel sounds of **a** and **o**, listed in the above paragraph, are easier to see in the mirror because our mouths open naturally to produce the sounds of **a** and **o**. With the mouths open, the students will be better able to see their tongues pressing to the back of their mouths. The instructor should encourage the students to freeze the **ng** sound and hold the sound for a long time, so they can see the tongue staying at the back.

Worksheet

Ready-to-Use Pictures for Digraph Letters

The diagraph letter pictures can be enlarged for making worksheets, classroom charts, and cards for sorting.

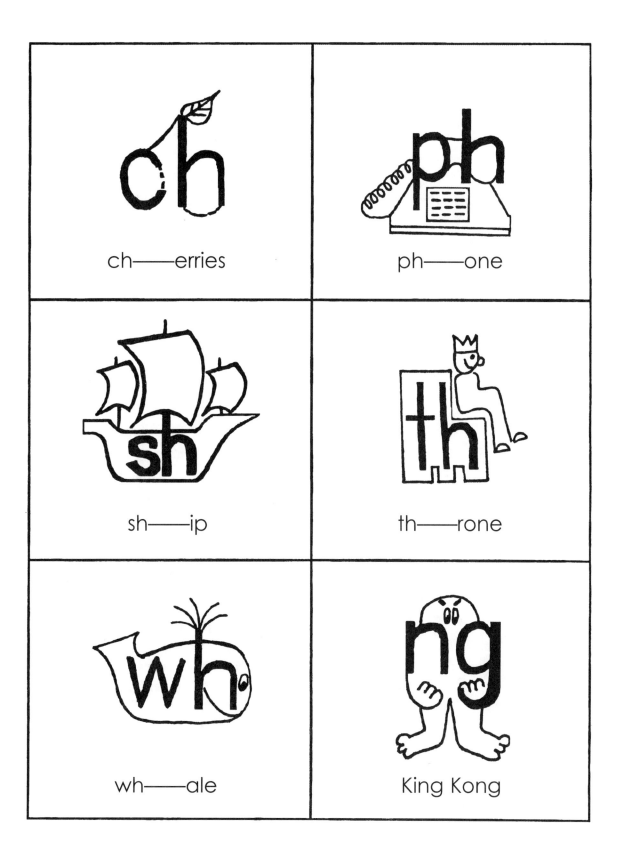

ch—erries

ph—one

sh—ip

th—rone

wh—ale

King Kong

◆▸ Strategy 4-3: Breaking Words into Smaller Chunks "chunk it"

Observed Behavior

Anna Bell successfully learned the individual sounds for all consonant and digraph letters. She can say the sounds for each letter while figuring out a word. However, by the time she gets to the end of the word, she is unable to remember the letters she started with; thus, she is unable to blend them together into the word.

Anna Bell is having difficulty with auditory memory when she must remember sounds in a specific order. This is confusing to her teacher, who knows that Anna Bell was very successful with learning the individual letter sounds through her auditory memory. Although Anna Bell can use her auditory memory, there is a limit to the number of sounds she can "hold" in her auditory memory bank. The amount of sounds or words we can hold at one time is called our *auditory memory span*. Anna Bell's auditory memory span is strong up to three or four sounds, depending on where the letters are placed in the word. But when she hits the fourth or fifth letter, she begins to get confused and loses sounds from her memory bank. How can we help Anna Bell use her shortened auditory memory span and still figure out words successfully? How can we teach her to systematically break words into smaller parts? How can we teach her to blend the smaller parts into the whole word she is attempting to figure out? How can we teach her to recognize word patterns that appear repeatedly in many words?

Strategies and Tools to Improve the Student's Performance

Let's assume that Anna Bell has mastered the concept of consonant "blend" sounds due to her ability to blend up to three letter sounds. So she knows how to "slide" two regular consonant sounds together to produce what is called a blended consonant. Many blends that come at the front of a word are formed with a consonant + **l** (for example: *bland, climb, flank*). Some are made with a consonant + **r** (for example: *brand, crack, drain*). Some consonant blends contain three letters (for example: *street, stretch, strain*). Anna Bell should be able to sound these "blend" parts easily because they never contain more than three letters.

Let's also assume that Anna Bell can recognize the vowel letters (a-e-i-o-u) and has mastered the essential concept for words, which states that all words must contain at least one vowel sound. Based on these two premises, we can begin teaching her how to break up single-syllable words.

First, we must teach Anna Bell how to break a word in front of the vowel letter to separate the beginning, or initial, sounds from the vowel "chunk" of the word. She must be very careful to check letter order from left to right because some vowels change sounds when they are in specific positions. (An example would be the word "grand." When the "r" follows a vowel, it changes the vowel sound from a short sound to an r-control sound.) Given the word "grand," which contains five sounds, Anna Bell will need to break up the word by making a cut in front of the vowel to separate the "gr" from "and."

Second, we must teach her to sound out the two small chunks. It is advisable to teach her to sound out the vowel chunk first. She should be encouraged to cover up the initial blend letters so she can focus on the vowel chunk "and" hiding in the whole word "grand."

Last, Anna Bell should slide the smaller chunk "gr" together with the "and" to hear "grand."

1. Use the recipe that follows to instruct students in "chunking" or breaking up a single-syllable word into smaller parts. Instruct students to:

- Look at the letters in the word from left to right.
- Find the first vowel. (*Optional:* Cut the word in front of the vowel.)
- Cover all the letters in front of the vowel with your fingers.
- Sound out the vowel part of the word you can see.
- Say the vowel chunk of the word.
- Lift your fingers and blend the sounds in the first part of the word.
- Say the initial chunk and blend it with the vowel chunk.
- Say the whole word.

2. Use a CUE CARD to illustrate the strategy for breaking a word into smaller chunks. The following card could be used to remind the students to use "chunking." It could be placed on the students' desks, on a bulletin board, or in a book as a reminder.

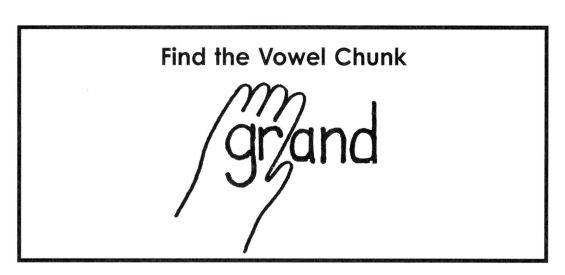

To make sure that Anna Bell understands how to break a word by cutting it in front of the vowel to get two parts, we should start with words that contain only short vowels. Short-vowel words have one vowel that is "closed in" by one or more consonant letters that follow the vowel in the word. Using the code **vowels = V** and **consonants = C**, a short-vowel word can look like **-VC** or **-VCC**. The empty spaces in front of the vowel would be the consonant blend sounds at the front of the word. Anna Bell can easily demonstrate her ability to recognize the short-vowel parts of words by completing worksheets that ask her to cut printed words into chunks. When Anna Bell is finished with a vowel "cutting" task, she should read the words to an adult to make sure she can pronounce the five (a-e-i-o-u) short sounds.

3. Use this sample task to model how to cut words into vowel "chunks." This task contains only short vowel "chunk" words. It can be used as a guide for developing additional worksheets for the other vowel "chunk" sounds. Word lists can be used to select new words, but the instructions remain the same.

CUTTING WORDS TO FIND VOWEL CHUNKS

1. Look carefully at each word.
2. Find the FIRST vowel.
3. Make a CUT LINE in front of that vowel.
4. Sound out the part after the cut mark.
5. Blend the letter sounds at the beginning of the word.
6. Say the whole word.

sw|ish	lunch	block	pinch	check
slash	ranch	chest	think	chops
fresh	mumps	stock	flint	bench
notch	chick	spots	blush	stomp
chuck	trick	speck	clamp	craft

What if the vowel part in a word contains <u>more than one vowel letter</u> (examples: fl<u>oa</u>t, br<u>ea</u>k, tr<u>ou</u>t, sp<u>oo</u>k)? Does Anna Bell know these double-letter vowel patterns? What if the vowel letters are spread out in the word (examples: stri<u>de</u>, fl<u>ame</u>, sm<u>oke</u>)? Does Anna Bell know these vowel patterns? When a word is broken into parts, the ending vowel part can also be called the *vowel pattern*. To ensure that Anna Bell is successful with chunking, or breaking up, words that contain variations in vowel patterns, we need to provide a system for recognizing vowel patterns that are seen repeatedly in words.

Instead of checking Anna Bell's skills one vowel pattern at a time—for example, all the "and" words, then the "ant" words, then the "ang" words, and so on—we should show her the most global organizational strategy for understanding vowel patterns. So, we will start with the six basic categories of vowel patterns used in single-syllable words. The six patterns actually define how most vowels will be pronounced based on where the vowels sit inside the word. Should Anna Bell have difficulty with any of the six basic categories, we can break it down further into the specific sounds for that group. (An example of further breakdown will be included for Anna Bell in this strategy section.) If Anna Bell were permitted to have a list, illustrations, or chart available for the six vowel patterns, she could always check her own accuracy when breaking down a word.

4. Use this chart for the six basic vowel patterns for single-syllable words in verbal and visual format. The chart can be used as a CUE CARD or an instructional concept card. Note that the blank spaces (boxes) preceding the **V**—for Vowel—stand for the letter or letters that would come at the beginning of the word in front of the vowel pattern.

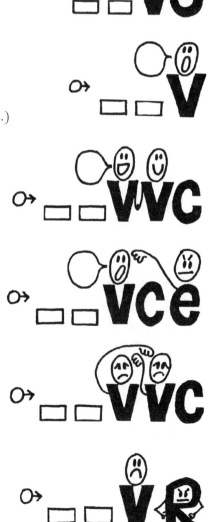

- "closed-in vowel"
  a vowel that has a consonant after it; therefore, it will have a **short sound**

- "open vowel"
  a vowel at the end of a word or syllable with no consonant closing it in; therefore, it will have a **long sound**
  (*Note:* Pattern is difficult in multisyllables.)

- "two vowels together"
  a pair of vowels "go walking, so the first one does the talking"; therefore, they will have a **long sound**

- "two vowels split by a sound"
  first vowel gets *bopped* by the last vowel, so the first one screams out its name; therefore, they will have a **long sound**

- "two vowels that don't play fair"
  two vowels that get in a fight and make a brand new sound; therefore, they will have a **diphthong sound**

- "one vowel followed by an R"
  one vowel controlled by "Bossy R," who forces the vowel to make a new sound; therefore, it will have an **r-control sound**

<u>Using sorting tasks</u> is another means of determining a student's skill with vowel sounds. These tasks can be done with word cards and the six category illustration cards, which can be found at the end of this strategy. However, most students initially benefit from breaking their tasks into a smaller number of categories. A logical first step would be to begin with only the short and long categories as students have likely had more exposure to these basic sounds.

5. Use the following sample cut-and-sort task to practice long- versus short-vowel words. Please note that this is a cut-and-sort task. Students will first need to cut out the boxes and then sort them under the correct vowel pattern illustration. (A full-page task is included at the end of this strategy section.)

Short Sounds ▫▫VC	Long Sounds ▫▫V	Long Sounds ▫▫VVC	Long Sounds ▫▫VCe
swish	train	she	stake
theme	fresh	screen	we

The next two patterns to be compared should be the "closed-in" short vowels versus r-control vowels, or "Bossy-R" vowels. Both of these patterns look the same, as they each contain one vowel letter. Yet the student must recognize that when the "r" letter is in a certain position, it can change the vowel noise. The "r" letter becomes powerful only when it sits exactly behind the vowel letter. When this happens, the vowel must make a different sound, which is called an "r-control." When completing the task, be sure the students read the words to an adult to make sure they are pronouncing the two types of sounds correctly.

6. Use the following sample task for sorting words with "closed-in" and "r-control" vowels. Please note that this is a cut-and-sort task. Students must be told to cut out all the word boxes and then sort them under the correct vowel/picture pattern. (A full-page task is included at the end of this strategy section.)

Closed Vowels Short Sounds	R-Control Vowels R-Sounds
VC	VR
chuck	shark
splash	perch
thirst	trench

The next two patterns to be compared and/or sorted should be the "two vowels together, that go walking" and the "two vowels together, that don't play fair." The two vowels that go "walking" are pronounced with regular two-vowel long sounds. The two vowels that "don't play fair" are diphthongs, which are irregular sounds. These patterns often look the same because they each contain two vowel letters. Yet the student must recognize when the two vowels do not play fair. It is essential that the students read the words to an adult to make sure they are pronouncing the two types of sounds correctly.

7. Use the following sample sorting task for regular "two-vowel long" and "two-vowel diphthong" vowels. Please note that this is a cut-and-sort task. Students must be told to cut out all the word boxes and then sort them under the correct vowel/picture pattern. A full-page task is included at the end of this strategy section.

2-Vowels Walking Long Sounds	Diphthong Vowels Diphthong Sounds
brain	greed
speech	join
throat	toys

Anna Bell encountered difficulty with the diphthong vowel sounds, so she will need further instruction on sounds for **au-aw**, **ou-ow**, **oi-oy**, and **oo-oo**. We need to supplement her global organization system of the six basic categories for vowel patterns with more detailed information for the diphthongs. She will need to learn the sounds that match the diphthong letters. We will switch to teaching the diphthong sounds through pictures that match the shape of the letters. Although there are eight general diphthong vowel sound pictures, it is best to introduce one pair of pictures at a time. The pairs are **au/aw**, **ou/ow**, **oi/oy**, and **oo/oo**. Anna Bell should name, trace, and freeze the picture words.

However, since Anna Bell has shown good auditory memory skills for most letter sounds, she may only need practice with real words that are sorted under each diphthong picture. When two pairs of diphthong pictures have been reviewed, Anna Bell could sort words. She may benefit from completing some of the steps for (1) naming the pictures, (2) tracing the letters/pictures, (3) printing the words for pictures, (4) breaking the words, and (5) freezing the words to hear/feel the vowel sounds of the picture words. Please refer to the recipe included with the first strategy in this section on pages 229 and 230, as it provides a general guide for introducing letter pictures and sounds.

8. Use the following illustrations for the irregular diphthong vowel sounds. An enlarged set is included at the end of this strategy section.

"au" . . . when I
pat the bunny

"ou" . . . I say
ouch, I got poked

"oi" . . . I see oil
in the can

"aw" . . . gee whiz,
I dropped my
ice cream

"ow" . . . I see
a cow

"oy" . . . I see a
boy doing a flip

"oo" . . . boo says
the ghost

"oo" . . . I can look
in a book

9. Use the sample word lists for sorting each type of diphthong vowel. The words can also be sorted with the illustrations for vowel patterns.

au – aw		ou – ow		oi – oy		oo – oo	
cause	thaw	pound	clown	point	Troy	bloom	shook
haul	straw	ground	crowd	moist	joy	choose	stood
fault	lawn	flour	frown	choice	boy	droop	crook
vault	shawl	mount	scowl	spoil	toys	roost	woods
Paul	squawk	slouch	plow	joint	ploy	groove	hooks

Once Anna Bell has demonstrated good ability to break up single-syllable words, she will be ready for instruction on how to break up <u>multisyllable</u> words. As a first step, she should be shown how prefixes and suffixes, many of which she already knows, can be added to root words to make bigger words. These bigger words are not hard for her to figure out because she can cover the prefixes and suffixes. With reminders to cover the added parts, she can concentrate on the root word and apply her "chunking" skills.

10. Use an updated CUE CARD as a reminder to cut big words into chunks. This card includes reminders to cover prefixes and suffixes and break larger words into smaller pieces to improve multisyllable-word decoding.

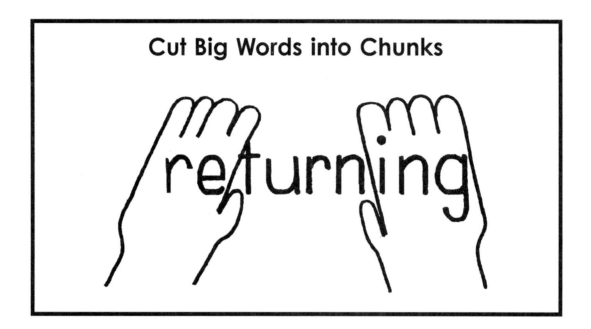

This strategy was chosen to demonstrate the importance of selecting the most global organizational system for the student's current skill levels. Anna Bell had already learned the consonant sounds, digraph sounds, and most of her vowel sounds through her auditory memory strength. By observing her difficulty with figuring out unknown words, the instructor could see that she was partially able to use her auditory memory, but it failed her beyond four sounds in a sequence. Anna Bell needed to keep using her auditory memory but in smaller pieces. By providing her with a general strategy of "chunking" and the six basic categories for vowel patterns, Anna Bell could decode most unknown words with accuracy. Only in one category, the diphthongs, did she need to have the global strategy of "six basic categories of vowel patterns" broken down. A supplemental step was needed to master these irregular sounds. She did not need a complete breakdown for individual vowel patterns in all the categories. If Anna Bell had been forced to review all the patterns, it would have wasted valuable learning time.

Worksheets

Ready-to-Use Set of Cards
for the Six Basic Vowel Patterns

The illustrations for vowel patterns can be copied and/or enlarged for creating worksheets, sorting tasks, and charts to which students can refer. You will notice there are two sets of cards. One set contains the basic category illustration. The other set includes the vowel letters and category information.

 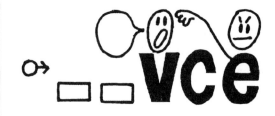

Closed-in Vowels
Short Sounds

Open Vowels
Long Sounds

2 Vowels Together
Long Sounds

2-Vowel BOPPERS
Long Sounds

2 Vowels Don't Play Fair
au/aw   ou/ow
oi/oy   oo/oo

Bossy R-Vowels
ar   er   ir   or   ur

Worksheets

Ready-to-Use Sorting Task for Vowel Chunk Patterns

Four "cutting" tasks with specific types of vowel patterns are included. These are:

- words that contain *only* single-vowel short vowel sounds
- words with short and long vowel patterns
- words with one vowel (short and r-control vowels)
- words with two vowels (long and diphthong vowels)

Each task asks the student to (1) cut out all the boxes and (2) sort the words under the correct vowel/picture pattern card.

	script	stock	cluck
	lunch	craft	speck
	trench	ditch	stomp
	block	slush	ranch
	splash	fresh	swish

Short Sounds	Long Sounds	Long Sounds	Long Sounds
_ _ VC	_ _ V	_ _ VVC	_ _ VCe
swish	train	she	stake
theme	fresh	screen	we
go	roast	stripe	ranch
snore	hi	trust	spray

Closed Vowels Short Sounds	R-Control Vowels R-Sounds
__ __**VC**	__ __**VR**
chuck	shark
splash	perch
thirst	trench
ditch	storm
stomp	church
burst	craft
fresh	twirl

2-Vowels Walking Long Sounds	Diphthong Vowels Diphthong Sounds
brain	greed
speech	join
throat	toys
slouch	scream
scowl	brook
peach	vault
crawl	cloak

Worksheet

Ready-to-Use Illustrations for the Diphthong Vowels

The illustrations for the irregular diphthong vowels can be copied and/or enlarged for creating worksheets, sorting tasks, and charts to which students can refer.

Diphthong Vowels

"aw" . . . gee whiz, I dropped my ice cream

"oo" . . . boo says the ghost

"oo" . . . I can look at a book

"au" . . . when I pat the bunny

"ow" . . . I see a cow

"oy" . . . I see a boy doing a flip

"ou" . . . I say ouch when I get poked

"oi" . . . I see oil in the can

❯ Strategy 4-4: "Going to the Bank" Script for Multiplication "talk it"

Observed Behavior

Henri is staring at a multidigit multiplication problem on his paper. He has written the steps for the first multiplier. Yet, when he started to do the next multiplier, he paused as if he was unsure. He started to whisper to himself as he tried to figure it out. Now he is sitting totally still with a grimace on his face. He does not know what to do next.

Henri is stuck. He can't proceed because he is confused by all the numbers in the multidigit multiplication problem and does not know what number he is supposed to use next. When his teacher asks him what he thinks he should do next, his response is, "I know I'm supposed to multiply these top numbers again, but I'm not sure how to do it." The sequence of steps for completing the problem is not clear for Henri. From his response to the teacher's question, Henri obviously does not understand the reasoning behind "why" the problem is done in a specific order.

Strategies and Tools to Improve the Student's Performance

Henri must see and participate in an activity that shows the action of multidigit multiplication to better understand the language of multiplication. Even though he does attempt to "whisper" or talk his way through the problem, he remains confused by the visual numbers on the page.

First, Henri must be helped to see what the sign and numbers in a sample multiplication problem mean in general. He will need to understand it in a way that is more meaningful to him.

Second, Henri must find another technique for monitoring the steps in multidigit multiplication. He may be more successful using his verbal memory skills with a script for the sequence once the process is meaningful to him.

Third, we can animate the problem by showing people "going to the bank." We can add stick-figure people and a bank to illustrate it. Doing this will allow Henri to visualize the scene because he has probably gone to the bank with his parents. Keep in mind, though, that this activity does not explain the step-by-step calculation sequence for working the problem. It will, however, help Henri to better understand the reasoning behind the multiplication process.

In the demonstration, we will use the sample problem 12 × $345. The following instructional illustration can be copied, enlarged, and/or made into an overhead for the instructor's use. Please note that the illustration includes all the completed steps, so the instructor may want to erase the "going to the bank" lines and totals for use with the students.

1. Use the completed illustration shown here to teach students the language used in the general multiplication process.

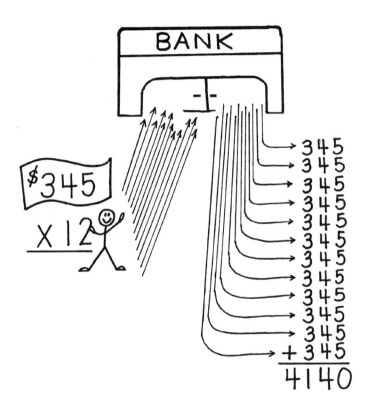

In parallel with the illustration, the instructor will need to point to and explain that the number that sits next to the "×" sign tells students how many "times" they get to "go to the bank." So, in this problem, they can go to the bank twelve times, because the 12 sits next to the "×" sign. The number at the top means how much money the bank is going to give the students "each time they come to the bank." So, in this problem, they can get $345 each time they go to the bank.

The instructor will need to demonstrate the twelve "trips to the bank" by drawing a line starting near the number 12, going into the bank and coming out with the $345 each time. After each trip, the $345 should be written in the column until all twelve trips are completed. The numbers can then be added to show the total is actually 4,140.

After such a long, complex demonstration, the instructor could reasonably comment, "A long time ago this is how they had to do the math to figure out how to get a total for big sets of numbers. Would you like to see a quicker way to get the same answer?"

2. Use the completed sequence shown here for <u>multiplying by the ones digit</u>.

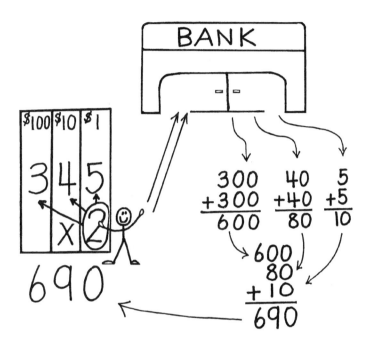

In parallel with the illustration, the instructor must demonstrate the next step of going to the bank with only one number at a time. Pointing to the 2 in the multiplier, circle it and say, "We are only getting money for the 'two times to the bank' part, so we are only multiplying 2 × 345." The instructor will need to include words to describe the kind of currency the bank will give for the ones, tens, and hundreds columns. **Say:**

"First, the bank will give us 5 one-dollar bills for each of our 2 times going to the bank, so 5 + 5 = 10." The instructor then lets the students get the bills out of a play money kit, so they can experience gathering the amounts.

"Next, the bank will give us 4 ten-dollar bills for each of our two times, so 40 + 40 = 80."

"Third, the bank will give us 3 one-hundred-dollar bills for each of our two times, so 300 + 300 = 600."

Last, "All of the money from the ones, tens, and hundreds added together will make $690. We can write that number under the multiplication problem. But we are not done; we only had 2 times to the bank and the problem said we could go to the bank 12 times. How many trips are left? Right! The bank still owes us 10 more times to the bank."

3. Use the completed sequence shown here for <u>multiplying by the tens digit</u> of a two-digit multiplier.

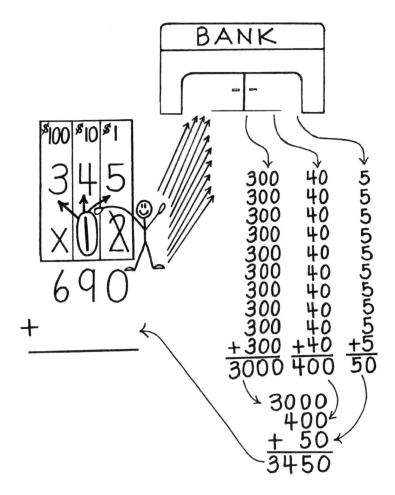

Again in parallel with the illustration, the instructor should circle the 1 in the multiplier, saying, "We are already done with the 2, so let's cross it out. We can write in the 690 for the 2 times part. Remember that this number 1 is really not a one; it actually represents a 10 because it sits in the tens place. So, when we go to the bank, we are actually getting ten each time from the banker. The rule is we have to get the 'cash' in the ones place first, then the tens, and last the hundreds." Let the students get the bills out of a play money kit.

Say: "So this time we go ten times for our piles of money. First, the bank will give us 5 one-dollar bills for each of our ten times going to the bank, so $5 + 5 + 5 + 5 + 5 + 5 + 5 + 5 + 5 + 5 = 50$."

"Next, the bank will give us 4 ten-dollar bills for each of our ten times going to the bank, so $40 + 40 + 40 + 40 + 40 + 40 + 40 + 40 + 40 + 40 = 400$."

"Last, the bank will give us 3 one-hundred-dollar bills for each of our ten times going to the bank, so $300 + 300 + 300 + 300 + 300 + 300 + 300 + 300 + 300 + 300 = 3000$."

"All of the money from the ones, tens, and hundreds added together will make $3,450. We can write this number in the problem. Remember to write the numbers in the right columns. The first number—$690—is the money from our 'two times to the bank.' The second number—$3,450—is the money from our 'ten times to the bank.' We have to add the numbers together to get the total for all the trips to the bank. The total would be $4,140. That matches the answer we got on the first way we did it."

Now, announce to the students, "That way still took too long. Would you like to see the easiest way to do multiplication?"

At this stage, Henri should be ready to see and understand the step-by-step sequence on paper for completing a multiplication problem with a two-digit multiplier. The instructor should describe each step as the numbers are marked. Keep in mind that this instruction will become a script, so use such words as *first, second, next, last*, etc. The instructor could choose to write lines of script as he or she works the problem and return to the script to review the entire sequence.

It is helpful to let the student do the written problem in parallel with the instructor modeling it. In a classroom, the teacher could do the problem on an overhead. The grid used for instruction (see illustration below) is completed for the entire process. It is easily adapted for direct use with a student. A suggested instruction recipe follows the illustration.

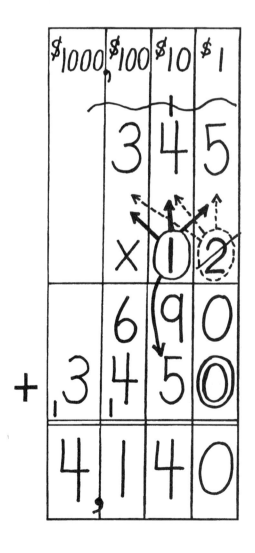

4. Use this recipe to instruct students about multidigit multiplication, using the preceding model. Say:

- "Find the ones number in the multiplier. Circle it. Did you circle the 2?"

- "First, go to the ones place for '2 times 5' = 10. Move your pencil point up to the 5, so you know which number you are using. Write the 0 and carry the 1 up to the next column because it is a ten."

- "Next, go to the tens for '2 times 4' = 8, but there is a 1 we carried, so we have 8 + 1 = 9. Write the 9 with nothing to carry."

- "Last, go to the hundreds for '2 times 3' = 6, and there is nothing carried, so we write 6."

- "We are done with the '2 times multiplier,' so cross it out. We are also done with the carrying numbers, so cross them out."

- "Ready? Now find the tens number in the multiplier. Circle it. Did you circle the 1? Remember the '1' is in the tens place, so we write the answer in the tens. Just so we don't forget, we'll always put a zero down below in the ones place."

- "First, go to the ones for '1 times 5' = 5. It should really be '10 times 5' = 50, so we need to write the 5 down in the tens place."

- "Next, go to the tens for '1 times 4' = 4. Write the 4 in the hundreds column, because it really would be '10 times 40' = 400. Check to be sure the 4 is in the hundreds column where it should be."

- "Last, go to the hundreds for '1 times 3' = 3. Write the 3 in the thousands column, because it really would be '10 times 300' = 3000. Be sure the 3 is in the thousands column, where it should be."

- "We're all done with the '1 times' multiplier, so cross it out."

- "Now, we get the total by adding the '2 times total' with the '1 times total.' Draw a line and add the numbers together to get the answer."

The instructor could then review and write a script on the board for all the students to see and follow. (The script that follows will rapidly decrease in length as it is practiced.)

5. Use this script to instruct students in multidigit multiplication with three-digit numbers. Say:

- "Circle the ones multiplier number."

- "First, multiply it times the ones, write the answer, carry any extra digit."

- "Next, multiply it times the tens, add on carried numbers, write the answer."

- "Last, multiply it times the hundreds, add on carried numbers, write the answer, but don't carry."

- "I'm done with the first multiplier, cross it out, cross out the carried numbers."

- "Circle the tens multiplier number, put in a zero to fill the ones below."

- "First, multiply it times the ones, write the answer in the tens, carry to next column."

- "Next, multiply it times the tens, add on any carried number, write the answer, carry to next column."

- "Last, multiply it times the hundreds, add on any carried number, write the answer, but don't carry."

- "Finally, add these two big numbers to get the answer."

Henri should be encouraged to practice his "script" while working problems. Over time, his script will decrease in length as he masters the sequence. Some students benefit from using their pencil as a pointer as they say their script. Such students usually decrease their need for "whispering" their script, because their pencil is reminding them of where to go next. Ask them which way they like to do it. Henri is an actual student who learned this script strategy, so you may enjoy his reduced but effective script, which is reproduced below. Notice that he keeps saying "this"; he does so because he is pointing and sometimes making lightly marked lines to the numbers he is multiplying with during the entire process. He was asked to talk the script aloud, but he explained that he prefers to do it silently while he looks at his pencil.

Here is Henri's personalized script.

- Circle the first multiplying number.
- Multiply it with this number.
- Next, multiply it with this number.
- Last, multiply it with this number.
- Cross out the multiplier and carried numbers.
- Circle the new multiplier.
- Write in the zero.
- Multiply it with this number.
- Next, multiply it with this number.
- Last, multiply it with this number.
- Finally, add.

The strategies in this section were selected to purposely demonstrate two means of organizing instruction for a student. Henri needed a real-life meaningful organization strategy to see how the process of multidigit multiplication actually worked. But he couldn't remember the steps visually when he was faced with "big number" problems. He needed an additional verbal organization strategy called a *script*, which used his verbal memory skills.

Worksheets

Multidigit Multiplication

The following worksheets purposely contain a completed model problem with which students can monitor their accuracy. The first sheet has one blank problem grid and the second sheet has three.

Name_____ **Date**_____

$1000	$100	$10	$1
	3	4	5
×	①	⟨2⟩
6	9	0
+3	4	5	⓪
4	1	4	0

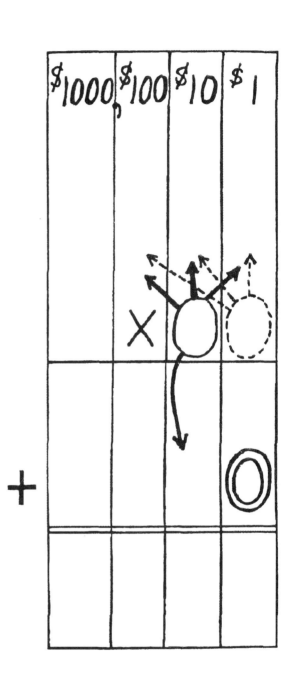

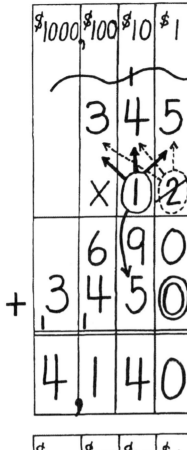

$1000,	$100	$10	$1
	3	4	5
×		①	⓶
	6	9	0
3,	4	5	⓪
4,	1	4	0

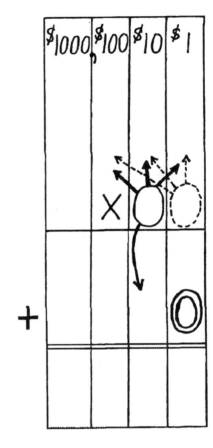

$1000,	$100	$10	$1
×			
			⓪
+			

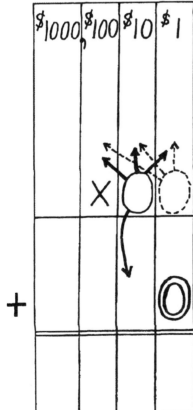

$1000,	$100	$10	$1
×			
			⓪
+			

$1000,	$100	$10	$1
×			
			⓪
+			

Strategy 4-5: Visual Layout for Long Division

"act it out"

Observed Behavior

Audrey is trying to work a long division problem on her paper. Although her teacher knows Audrey has mastered the concepts for multiplication and subtraction and understands the basic concept of simple division, all skills that are needed in long division, she knows Audrey is struggling. Every time Audrey does the first step of long division, trying to "fit in" the divisor into the total amount, she delays because she does not know where to write the numbers or how to go to the next step.

Audrey has mastered most of the basic skills that are required for the complex process for long division, but she gets lost in the sequencing of the steps. Audrey has attempted to memorize "what" to do in the long division process without understanding the mathematical reasoning for "why" it only works in a specific order. She does not understand that the basic purpose of division is to "take out," or subtract, sets from a larger quantity, so everyone involved ends up with a fair share. Without understanding the "why," she is unable to remember "how" to do it. How do we help her see the division of a large quantity into smaller equal sets?

Strategies and Tools to Improve the Student's Performance

1. Provide a meaningful visual layout for the parts of long division. Audrey needs to begin to understand why long division works the way it does. She'll need specific materials to represent the parts. The following would be helpful: (1) a division grid (illustrated next), (2) a money kit, (3) a set of number cards, and (4) a set of baskets to separate each share of the total money.

As instructors, we must make the numbers meaningful to students. Audrey must see and hear the mathematical language of long division so it makes sense. For example, in the problem 725 divided by 5, you could show that the 5 could be 5 people and the 725 could be the money that must be shared equally. Audrey must also understand that specific currency matches each number in $725. The correct currency could be placed under or next to each number on the division grid that is divided into three sections for the hundreds, tens, and ones. The divisor "5 people" could then be placed outside the long division sign that encloses the $725. Each of the "5 people" could be represented by individual baskets. The instructor would then be ready to demonstrate the active process of separating larger amounts of money into smaller but equal sets so everyone gets their fair share.

Use the following illustration to demonstrate the visual layout of numbers and currency in long division.

2. Have students lay out materials on a tabletop, using the illustration as a guide. Audrey can participate in "taking out" equal sets of currency and giving them to each of the 5 people. It is essential for her to understand that the currency available often cannot be shared equally. Demonstrate with simultaneous pointing to numbers and moving money as you describe the process.

Say: "Watch me. Here are the 5 people. They are walking inside the division mark to see how much money there is. They stop at the hundreds first and see there are 7 hundred-dollar bills. The 5 people ask each other if there is enough for everyone. Will 5 'fit into' 7? How many 'times' will 5 fit in? It fits in 'one time,' so each person will only get one in their basket. We take 5 away from the 7, so there will be 2 hundreds left that cannot be shared equally."

3. Teach students that the "leftover" hundreds must be exchanged for smaller currency and used in the next "taking out" step. All students chuckle when it is suggested that maybe they could simply tear the bills into pieces. They realize they must go to the bank and trade in the hundreds for tens. The instructor must demonstrate changing the 2 "leftover" hundred-dollar bills for 20 ten-dollar bills. The students can then see they have 20 tens (received from trading in the 2 hundreds) plus the 2 tens still sitting in the division sign. Now they have 22 tens that must be shared equally by 5 people. See the next illustration for the visual layout of this step.

This illustration demonstrates the process of changing hundred-dollar bills for tens.

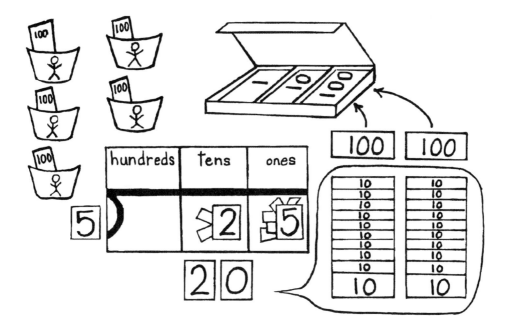

Once again, the instructor must simultaneously point to specific numbers as he or she describes the process.

Say: "Can you see that we now have the 20 tens we got by changing in the 2 extra hundreds plus the 2 tens here in the money we started with in the division problem? We now have 22 tens for 5 people to share. Does 5 'fit into' 22? Sure, but 'how many times' does it fit in equally for everyone? How many can we put in each basket? We can use multiplication to know $5 \times 4 = 20$, and it can't be 5×5 because there are not 25 to share. So, we'll give each person 4 ten-dollar bills." (Pick up the 22 ten-dollar bills and distribute them equally to each of the five baskets.) "We took away 20 ten-dollar bills, so there are 2 tens left."

4. Teach students that the "leftover" ten-dollar bills must be exchanged for one-dollar bills and distributed in the next step. The instructor would repeat the demonstration and change the 2 tens for 20 one-dollar bills. The 20 one-dollar bills combined with the 5 ones still sitting in the division sign (20 + 5) would then be distributed to the five baskets. The students could then see that each person would get 5 one-dollar bills, but this time none would be left over.

5. Have students determine the total amount of money that each person would receive. Audrey needs to determine how much money each of the 5 people would get. She would benefit from the opportunity to actually count each basket's contents to recognize that they all have the same amount. She could then recognize the total for each person would be $145. To be sure she got her fair share, she could add all the people's baskets, or 145 + 145 + 145 + 145 + 145 = 725. The total of the baskets must match the amount of money in the original division problem.

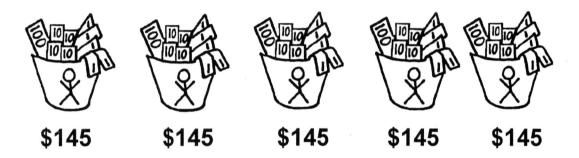

This strategy was selected to demonstrate how to break down a very complex process using a meaningful display of concrete materials. The visual layout enabled Audrey to see and participate in the action of division and experience the trading of larger currency for smaller but equal currency. By acting out the process, Audrey may be able to "re-imagine," or visualize, the experience each time she does a long division problem. She will now have a visual image in her mind with which she can monitor the accuracy of her work on paper.

◗ Strategy 4-6: Model Problem for Checking Long Division   "check it"

Observed Behavior

Ricky is a good math student. He understands all his basic concepts, but gets really confused when he has to do a problem with lots of details on the paper. He just can't remember where all the little things go or how to keep things in order. Whenever he tries to do a complex long division problem, he just can't keep track of the parts.

With structure, Ricky can tell his teacher exactly how to do a complex long division problem, yet when he tries to put it down on paper, he cannot do it accurately. He can use his words, or verbal memory, to tell how to do it, but he can't remember the visual details. He gets lost in knowing which column to put numbers in and confused on which number should be brought down next in the division problem. How can we help him?

Strategies and Tools to Improve the Student's Performance

1. Provide an interim strategy that might resolve some of the difficulty with column confusion. Normally, teachers ask students to do their written problems on lined paper, with the lines running across the page. This does not help Ricky. He needs to have visible columns in which to write his numbers. In the past, his teacher had suggested that he use graph paper, but it increased his visual confusion. Instead, the instructor should demonstrate how Ricky can turn his lined paper sideways, so he can write his numbers in the visible vertical columns.

Here's a sample problem completed on "turned sideways" lined paper.

$$
\begin{array}{r}
271 \text{ R}2 \\
23{\overline{\smash{\big)}\,6235}} \\
\underline{-46} \\
163 \\
\underline{-161} \\
25 \\
\underline{-23} \\
2
\end{array}
$$

2. Provide a model problem. Once Ricky can depend on his numbers being in the correct columns, he will be ready for the organizational strategy of using a model problem. Given a model against which he can check his own accuracy, Ricky will be able to independently monitor his own written work. He can then "talk" his way through the problems while looking at the model to check the accuracy of his talking. He may want to keep the model problem available in his book or notebook. However, he may be too embarrassed to use it in front of his peers, so would benefit from having a model problem mounted somewhere in the classroom. In this way, he could look at it without calling too much attention to his difficulty.

What needs to be included in the model division problem? The student must be able to recognize:

- the whole process
- the order of the essential steps
- the placement of the parts/details

To illustrate these three critical parts of a model, it is often helpful to add color-coded cues or graphic markings that emphasize important parts. A full-page enlargement of the model is included at the end of this strategy.

Here is a sample of Ricky's visible model for long division.

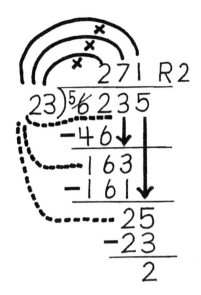

The highlighted <u>graphic cues</u> in the model problem must be clearly explained. For example, the dotted "walking" line from the divisor into the larger dividend number is meant as a visual reminder to first divide or "fit in" the divisor. The arch at the top of the problem connecting the "number of times it fits in" with the divisor is meant as a visual reminder to multiply. The subtraction marks are also highlighted as a reminder to subtract. The last major graphic cue is the vertical arrow that is meant as a visual reminder to bring down only one number to start the next set of steps. Notice that the "walking line," the "multiplication arch," the "bring-down" arrow, and the subtraction marks are repeated three times.

Although it cannot be seen in this black-and-white text, Ricky benefits from having these items <u>color-coded</u> for emphasis. The use of color is very effective for visual learners because it calls extra attention to those parts. For consistency, the "walking line" should be green; the arches, orange; the subtraction marks, blue; and the "bring down" arrows, red.

To ensure that the model problem is an effective tool for Ricky, the instructor also must <u>meet privately</u> with him to personalize it to his needs. The instructor would need to show and/or act out the model problem to be sure Ricky understands it. While explaining the visual model, be very observant of Ricky's subtle body reactions, because most students do not readily reveal their confusion. Should Ricky make subtle facial grimaces, the model could easily be changed for him.

This strategy was selected to demonstrate two organizational ideas. Some students need a small interim strategy to compensate for a minor difficulty before tackling a more significant learning problem. With Ricky's visual column difficulty reduced by the use of lined paper turned sideways, he was ready for a model. Students who get lost writing problems on paper can greatly benefit from the opportunity to compare their work against a model. Models can be created for all mathematical operations.

Worksheet

Model Problem for Checking Division

This sample problem can be enlarged for a chart or reduced for a CUE CARD to be placed on a student's desk or in a math book.

.

Model for Long Division

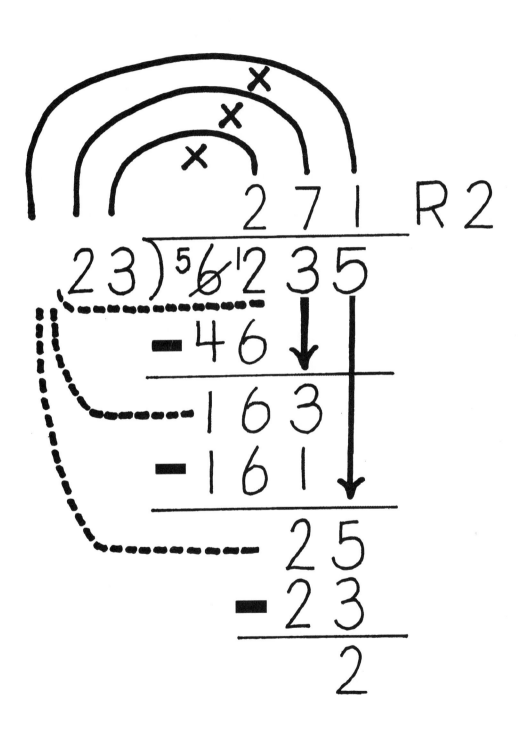

Strategy 4-7: Recipe for Long Division

"write the recipe"

Observed Behavior

Clara has successfully used the visual layout of baskets and money to comprehend the long division process. Her teacher has observed Clara stopping in the middle of doing a problem to look up at the model on the chart at the front of the room. Yet it doesn't seem to help her a lot because she has to spend a great deal of time comparing her problem to the one on the chart. Although Clara usually figures out a solution to her difficulty, it is becoming very frustrating, because she can't finish her paper as fast as the rest of the class does.

We know Clara understands the process of long division, but she is dependent upon the model problem on the chart with which she must compare her work to check its accuracy. In addition, she appears to be experiencing difficulty in analyzing the sequence on the model. Remember, she learned the process with the help of the visual baskets display; this indicates she is probably a visual learner. So, the chart is too sequential to be an efficient checking tool for her. How can we create a tool that is more visual to help her monitor the complex sequence, so she can become less dependent upon the chart model?

Strategies and Tools to Improve the Student's Performance

Before we can expect Clara to use another tool, we need to make sure she understands the five basic steps in the repeated pattern of long division. As instructors, we may need to use the chart model—which Clara seems to understand—to identify the five basic steps. Point to the numbers and markings written in the model problem. **Say:** "Let's look at the model. We need to find the five steps that are repeated over and over when we do division."

- **Then say:** "First, we 'fit in' the number, or <u>divide</u>."
- "Second, we figure out 'how many times,' or <u>multiply</u>."
- "Third, we 'take out' the total amount for all the guys, or <u>subtract</u>."
- "Fourth, we '<u>check it</u>' to make sure we took out enough."
- "Fifth, we '<u>bring down</u>' the next number in the division problem. And then we start all over again at the first step."

After identifying the five parts, the instructor should explain to students that they are going to <u>make a recipe</u> for long division that will make it easier to remember the steps. It may help students understand the importance of ordering steps by comparing the division recipe to a real cooking recipe. For example, if you put things in the bowl in the wrong order, you might not end up with a good cake.

How do we make an effective recipe for division? We must include each of the steps (Divide, Multiply, Subtract, Check, Bring Down), but we can simplify the recipe by using the first letter of each word—D-M-S-CH-B. If the students can remember the letters, they will be able to keep track of the sequence as they are working long division problems. The letters could be written at the top of the paper, so the student can look up and check the correct order as he or she works.

By themselves, the letters are hard to remember, so we must help the students to connect the letters to a meaningful association. However, each student needs to create an association that is personally memorable. The <u>association for a visual learner</u> would best be illustrated with pictures. So, Clara would imagine a series of pictures related to division. Clara might visualize or draw her sequence as "Daddy, Mommy, Sister, better Check it, says Brother, because she might cheat me out of my fair share." Clara could imagine a little sister trying to cheat her brother. Notice that Clara's visualization sentence includes words directly related to division by mentioning being cheated out of a fair share. Without this connection to division, Clara might not remember the letters for the steps. Also notice that Clara's drawing is very simple, so it can be easily copied.

1. Use this visual illustration for D-M-S-CH-B.

Do you remember Ricky in the previous strategy? He easily talked his way through division, using his verbal memory strength. Would he benefit from using the picture associations to improve his step-by-step accuracy in division?

The answer is probably yes, but we will need to adapt the <u>association for a</u> <u>verbal learner</u>. We'll use the same letters D-M-S-CH-B. However, for the verbal learner, the recipe would best be learned with words in a clever or unique way. So Ricky would use words that start with each letter—in order—to make a sentence. He would have to associate his sentence idea with something that has to do with division. Ricky imagined McDonald's as a place where he usually had to divide his burger and fries with his little brother. His sentence is as follows: "Does McDonald's Sell Cheese Burgers?"

Once the students have mastered their associations for the 5-step recipe, they will be able to remember the letters. The students will then be able to write the letters at the top of their papers, so they can consult it as they work problems. Should the students forget to write the "recipe" letters, the instructor could remind them, using the words "write the recipe" as a verbal cue. Or, the students could be reminded visually with an illustrated CUE CARD that is placed on the students' desk or in a math book.

2. Create CUE CARDS to illustrate the strategy for reminding the students to write the letters for the division recipe on their paper.

This strategy was selected to demonstrate how to develop an association for a complex sequence. The concept can be applied to all content areas.

☀ Strategy 4-8: Comic Strip Story Planner

"draw it"

Observed Behavior

Bret's assignment is to write a short paragraph about something he does at home. He has written his first sentence, telling about getting ready for school in the morning. After looking off in space for a long time, he finally writes two more sentences. His sentences simply list two steps he completes in the morning without providing any descriptive details. Even after the teacher suggests he include more words about what was happening, Bret was unable to add more sentences to his paragraph.

Bret tried to remember about his morning routine at home by looking off in space to recall specifics. Yet he was only able to remember two main events, eating and dressing, that he could "put into words" in sentences on his paper. Thinking in "words" is obviously difficult for Bret. He is struggling with verbal skills that require students to put ideas, or words, in a specific order to make sentences for a paragraph. Given the teacher's observation of Bret's struggle with written language, it would be reasonable to assume that he might benefit from experimenting with more visual approaches for writing. How do we begin when we know Bret did try to "look off in space" to remember? He may have been trying to re-imagine, or *visualize*, what occurs at home in the morning, but his attempts were not very successful. As a first step, we need to help Bret find a concrete way to see what he remembers, as he plans ideas for a written language task.

Strategies and Tools to Improve the Student's Performance

Students who have the potential to use their visual memory often need to learn how to activate the skill of visualizing, or imagining in the mind's eye. The simplest tool for learning to visualize is through drawing. As the students draw what they remember, they can come to "see" the visualization. The students are creating a representation on paper for what is stored inside their visual memory. Most students are initially very embarrassed by their drawings, so the instructor must be sure to explain that the quality of the drawing is not important. Students need to understand that the purpose of the drawing is to strengthen their ability to "paint" clear pictures or images, so they are more easily recalled. By being encouraged to draw, many students, over time, will be able to self-visualize without drawing.

1. Provide students with an easy-to-follow format for drawing. As most students enjoy the comics, they will understand the logic of laying out their ideas in a three- or four-fold horizontal string of boxes. The instructor can either suggest that they fold an unlined piece of paper into sections or provide a designed worksheet.

Here is a sample comic strip story planner.

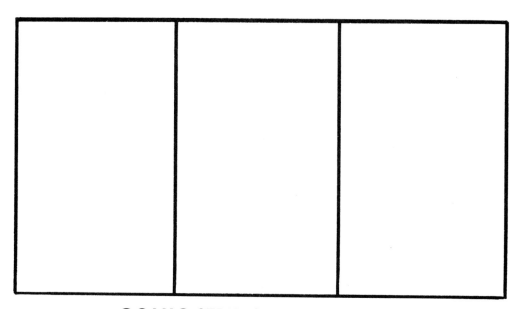

COMIC STRIP STORY PLANNER

2. Explain and/or demonstrate how to select a specific topic for the drawing. Given the horizontal (left-to-right) layout of the comic strip, Bret would be more aware of the need to order his events for each box. The instructor could encourage Bret to stop and think about the main settings to be drawn. Each section of the comic strip would become a scene from his morning routine. By drawing each scene, Bret would be able to "think back and recall through imagining it in his mind." The greater the amount of time a student spends on "thinking," usually the more amount of detail that appears within the comic strip sections.

However, if a student like Bret attempts to hurry through his drawing, he could be encouraged to add details with reminders to think more about "how it looks" in his scene. For example, in Bret's original story, his first sentence simply said, "I get up and eat breakfast." As he was drawing, Bret remembered—with some assistance—that he could add his favorite cereal box and juice. By adding these visual details to his drawing, he would be able to expand his sentences when he wrote about the "eating" section of his comic strip.

Initially, Bret had included only eating and dressing in his morning routine. Using the comic strip layout, he added two additional parts, watching television and hearing his mother call him when the bus came. With some encouragement, he added visual details such as the remote control, his sister sitting next to him, and their favorite show to the television scene. He also added the bus honking two times.

Here is a sample of Bret's completed comic strip worksheet.

3. Provide a visible format or structure to help students sequence their written sentences. With his drawing completed, Bret was ready for writing. Yet, as he had no guide for how to organize his sentences, he struggled to put the words down on paper. When students are first learning the basic rules of paragraph writing, they benefit from having an outline that includes the essential parts. A good paragraph has an introductory sentence, detail sentences, and a closing or summary sentence. The format presented to Bret included spaces in which he could write his sentences for each section of his comic strip to provide details about his morning as well as the introductory and closing sentences. Because his story included a specific sequence, the format also included sequential words such as *first*, *next*, and *last*. Bret called the worksheet a "story writing helper." Because the worry of spelling can limit the quality of sentence, Bret was told not to worry about spelling.

Here is Bret's completed rough draft on his paragraph guide form. A ready-to-use sample is included at the end of this strategy.

Paragraph Writing Guide

1. **Title:** _Getting Ready for School_

2. **Introductory Sentence: This story is about**
   getting ready in the morning

3. **FIRST part of the story**
   First I get up and eat my favorit ceral. I like ornge juce to.

4. **NEXT part of the story**
   Next me and my sister go to the living room to wach tv. I press the remote and change the chanel to the cartunes.

5. **LAST part of the story**
   Befor I go to school I put on my cloths. The bus pulls up and honks two times. My Mom yells "hurry up."

6. **Summary Sentence: (choose one)**
   I ~~am~~ _have to rush every day in the morning._
   I think _mornings are hard._

4. Support students by having them orally re-read their rough drafts to make sure they "sound" right and that all spelling, punctuation, and capital letters are correct. Spelling correction focused on Bret's ability to recognize when words looked "funny." If he could identify "funny words," he was given the correct spelling to copy. Errors in grammar were not addressed, as Bret had not received instruction on the use of pronouns (for example, *me* vs. *I*). Corrections were made on the rough draft before it was copied onto special paper that included an empty space for attaching his original comic strip.

5. To emphasize the value of writing, students' final draft stories can be collected and bound into "Short Story" volumes at the end of the year. In Bret's class, covers were designed, with professional-looking title pages identifying the student author. Some students wanted to start a special section in the library for "student authors."

Here is Bret's completed final draft.

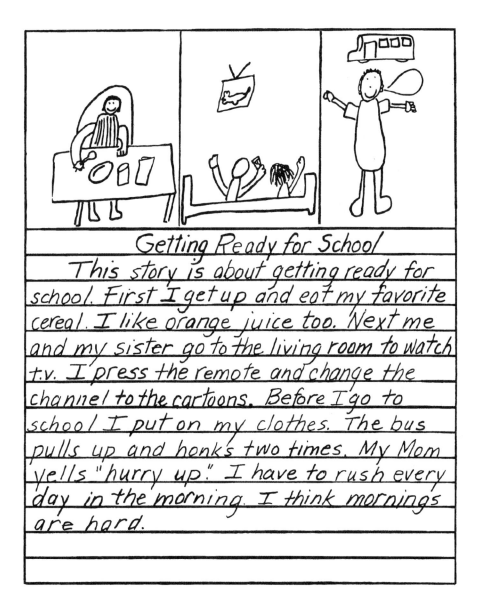

Worksheet

Comic Strip Story Planner

The following comic strip planner is provided as a convenience for the instructor. Although it could be created by simply folding a paper, students' exposure to a special form often increases the importance of planning ideas through drawing.

COMIC STRIP STORY PLANNER

Worksheet

Paragraph Writing Guide

The attached paragraph writing guide is provided as a convenience for the instructor. All emerging writers benefit from the availability of a visual guide for constructing logically ordered sentences on a topic.

Paragraph Writing Guide

1. Title: _____

2. Introductory Sentence: This story is about

_____

_____

3. {FIRST} part of the story

_____

_____

_____

4. {NEXT} part of the story

_____

_____

_____

5. {LAST} part of the story

_____

_____

_____

6. Summary Sentence: (choose one)

I am _____

_____

I think _____

_____

_____

Strategy 4-9: Visual Organizer for General Written Topic   "use the WH rule" "bubble sheet"

Observed Behavior

Pai is writing her response to an essay question on a social studies test. She obviously knows many facts about the Greenland Project, which is the topic of the question, but she does not put her ideas together in a logical order. She jumps from one fact to the next without thinking about how they are related.

Pai is a good student. She has studied and mastered the facts necessary to answer the essay question on the test. The question asks, "What is the Greenland Project and why was it attempted?" Still, she is unable to select and organize her known ideas into clusters that logically lead to the next point she wants to make in her response. How do we help plan her ideas so she is more prepared to write a clear response?

Strategies and Tools to Improve the Student's Performance

Planning for written language is a skill that can be learned, but students must have many opportunities to practice organizing their ideas. The most basic skill included in organizing language is the concept of categories. Given Pai's observed factual learning ability, we can assume that she has learned to categorize words into very complex categories. So, we can use this probable skill as a basis for showing her how to categorize her facts on a specific topic.

1. Give students six broad categories under which they can cluster their facts before attempting a written response. The categories are *who, what, when, where, why,* and *how.* Although we could verbally describe how each of Pai's facts could fit into one of these categories, it is more effective to show her a visual organizer that provides space for her to insert the facts. The organizer should also include a space to insert the title of the specific topic. For the sake of simplicity, this type of organizer is called the "WH organizer." (Visual learners often call it the "bubble sheet.") As some students resist this kind of strategy because it requires extra time, it may prove valuable to explain that the "Who, What, When, Where rule" has long been used by newspaper reporters to ensure that a story is accurately covered. Newspaper articles could be analyzed to verify the rule's use.

Here is a sample "WH organizer" or "bubble sheet." A full-page sample is included at the end of this strategy section.

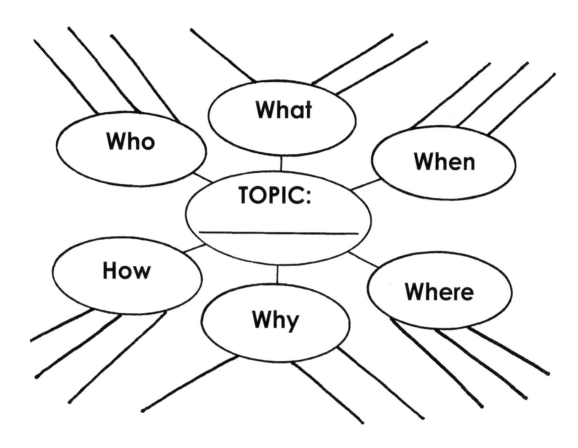

2. Show students how to fill in the visual organizer. Because Pai has never seen this tool before, it is important to remove the memory aspect of the task and permit her to use her text to locate the facts she wants to include in each "WH" category bubble. In the center bubble, she'll write the specific topic, "What is the Greenland Project and why was it attempted?"

Although the organizer is separated into six categories, Pai will complete it as a whole. So, as she re-scans her text for relevant facts, she will place them in varied areas depending on the category in which they would best fit. Notice that Pai has added words inside the "WH" category bubbles to further clarify the specific kind of facts that are included. She also has added extra fact lines, where needed, in specific category bubbles.

Here is Pai's completed "WH rule" visual organizer.

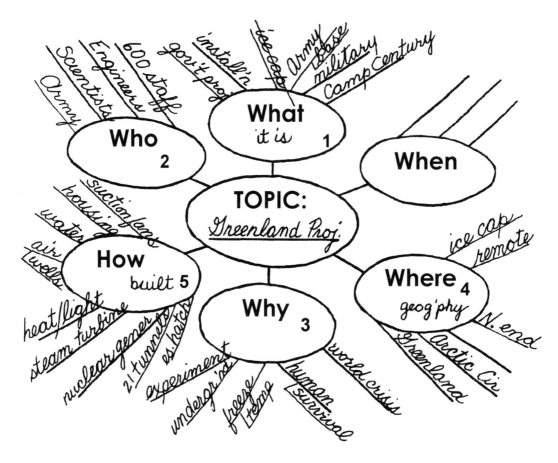

3. After they have completed the visual organizer, provide students with guidance on how to use the categories as they actually write their response to the question. The instructor should demonstrate how to mentally plan the logical order of the categories. It is essential to explain to students that they must not jump back and forth between categories if at all possible. However, while writing, they may discover that facts were placed in the wrong categories. Those facts can be moved. Pai did move one fact (ice cap) from the "what" category to the "where" category as can be seen on her organizer, where it is crossed out and rewritten.

In preparing to write, students should be instructed to select only their starting category initially. They must know that it is their personal choice. The visual organizer is not intended to set a required order. In Pai's completed organizer, notice that she wrote a "1" in the "what" category bubble. She felt it made more sense to tell what the project was first and then later go into the specific details that were found in the other category bubbles. Using the facts in the "what" category, she began her written response with:

The Greenland Project was actually a government-sponsored project.
It became a huge military installation later named Camp Century
Army Base.

After completing the first bubble, Pai couldn't decide which category to use next. The most difficult part of organized writing is <u>linking ideas together</u>. With encouragement to talk aloud in order to hear her thinking, Pai was able to recognize that it made more sense to write about the "who" for her "2" category. She noticed that her completed sentences discussed the military installation and this logically linked to specific people on the project. So she continued with:

> The base was staffed primarily with Army personnel. Eventually, more than six hundred men were needed to complete the project. In addition, there were highly trained engineers and scientists.

Using her talk-aloud strategy, Pai quickly recognized that the mention of "scientists" led logically to "why" they would be in Greenland. She continued with:

> The scientists collaborated with the Army in an experiment to determine if humans could survive in the extreme cold should a world disaster occur in more populated areas of the earth. The scientists and engineers developed plans for creating an underground base.

The mention of "underground base" led logically to a discussion of "where" the actual base was located. She continued with:

> The northern end of the island of Greenland was chosen as the site of the base. This area, located in the Arctic Circle region, was the most remote area of land available to test the premise of possible human survival in extreme temperatures. The base was built under a glacier ice cap where temperatures fell to 50 degrees below zero.

The mention of the "base" and the "ice cap" led logically to a discussion of "how" the base was built. She continued with:

> The base consisted of 21 underground tunnels for housing the staff. To survive underground, it was necessary to create an energy source with nuclear power and steam turbines. Special lighting was installed for underground life. Water was accessed through deep wells in the ground level of Greenland. Air was circulated through air wells and suction fans that extended to the surface of the ice cap. Escape hatches were constructed for emergency purposes. The installation included areas for staff living and entertainment.

Pai was pleased with her essay, but understood that it required an ending statement. She closed with:

> Although the experiment was a success and Camp Century still exists today, it is no longer in full operation. My hope is that I will never be forced to live under an ice cap. I can't imagine living in such a place.

Instructors should notice the numbered category bubbles that Pai used did not include the "when" bubble. That's because Pai appropriately determined that she did not need those facts to support her essay response. Students should be told that often all the bubbles are not used.

It is reasonable to expect that Pai would, over time, become less dependent upon filling in a visual organizer to answer an essay question. Instead, she could simply visualize the worksheet in her mind as she mentally organized her facts. She could imagine the logical numbering of each "bubble" category. In addition, she could "talk aloud" to hear her planning as she wrote.

However, even if students do not need to fill in the visual "bubble sheet," they may need to have their memory jogged every so often, so they will remember to organize their thoughts before beginning to write. It is helpful to place a CUE CARD in a visible place in the environment to trigger the use of the strategy.

4. Create visual CUE CARDS for planning ahead for written tasks.

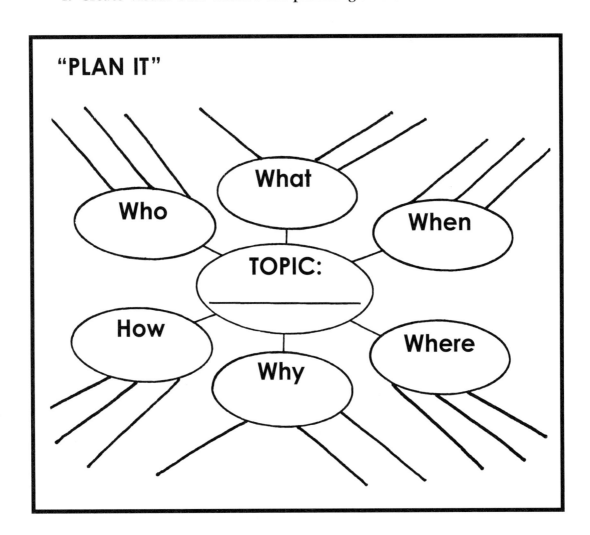

Worksheet

"WH" Visual Organizer

The following visual organizer is provided as a convenience for the instructor. Its use is easily demonstrated for all ages of students. Because of its very simple format, it can be adapted for all areas of content.

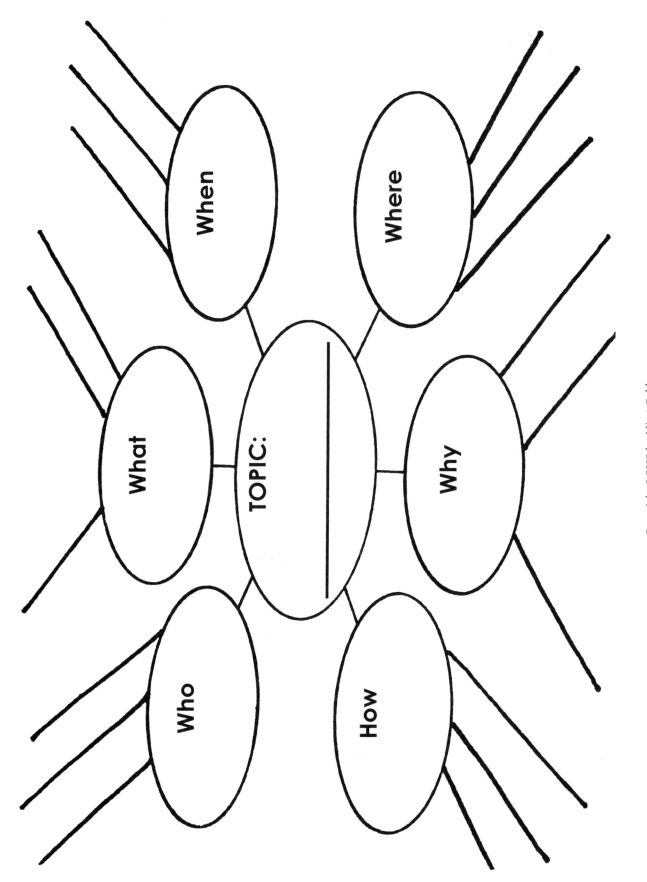